5/15/04

To Mar

Live What
You
Believe !

Tonya Kerry

Ephesians 3:20

TWELVE SECRETS
TO
LIVING A LIFE YOU LOVE

Tonya Kerri Johnson

ISBN 0-7414-0948-8

Published by:

INFI(∞)ITY
PUBLISHING.COM

1094 New Dehaven Street
Suite 100
West Conshohocken, PA 19428-2713
Info@buybooksontheweb.com
www.buybooksontheweb.com
Toll-free (877) BUY BOOK
Local Phone (610) 941-9999
Fax (610) 941-9959

Printed in the United States of America

Printed on Recycled Paper

Published April 2004

Contents

Acknowledgements

To My Mother:
For bringing me into this world - I am grateful to God for using you as the vessel.

To My Father:
Thanks for making things right. Hooray for whatever it is!

To Ramona:
For all that you are becoming. I love you.

To Tina & Richard:
Thanks for holding down the love! Stay strong.

To Jada & Anthony:
You are little angels. I love you too!

To Asha:
For laughing at my stories when you were three, and continuing to inspire and motivate me. I love you.

To My Friends:
Nicole, Mama Jo, Dawn, Glenda, Jean, Angelina, Keri, Bonnie & Linda:
You are real-life angels. I am honored to know you.

To My Godmother Rosa:
For supporting me when I was putting the pieces of myself back together again after little bits of me had been scattered all over the place.

To Les:
Here's to sweet potato pie!

To My Pastor Dr. Bernard:
You are a master teacher. Thank you.

To My Husband Derek:
For stepping up my love and being bold. Thanks. You are a 6'2" sack of sugar for sure! I love you more each day!

Most of All to God:
Thank you for never leaving me - Especially during the times when I thought you were not there. I now understand that you were simply busy working on my divine plan. Thank you Jesus!

Forward by Les Brown

Look out world, Tonya Kerri Johnson is here to resurrect those who have given up and allowed their dreams to die! Life is not easy. Sometimes it takes everything in you and more to keep your head up and smile. In addition, when you are aware there is a higher calling on your life, and you are living below your potential, it's brutal. Tonya has been there, done that, and bought the tee shirt. She decided this job is killing me, I can do better than this, and I've got to. Tonya took a deep breath, and with faith and courage decided to live the life she desired and felt passionate about. And along the way, like Hansel and Gretel, she left breadcrumbs of inspiration for those of us who desire to live a life of contribution, and dare to follow her example.

In this book, she takes you through a gut wrenching, agonizing experience that you will identify with, when you know in your heart of hearts that you are not happy with your life as it is. You're tired of pretending, and finally you say, "I've had it, I'm out of here -- see ya!"

Twelve Secrets to Living a Life You Love will give you the key to break out of your self-imposed prisons and set yourself free.

My youngest son John Leslie said in a speech recently, "You can't get out of life alive, so you might as well live while you're here." These pages will provide for you, tried and proven methods that Tonya and other top world achievers have used throughout history. While her secrets are common sense, they are not common practice. And please, don't permit the simplicity of her message to fool you into believing that it's easy to pursue a new life for yourself.

Tonya gives it to you straight, with no chaser. And if you're ready to discover the greatness you have within, to have more and to experience more, fasten your seat belt because you're about to soar to heights beyond your wildest dreams. Tonya is not only a gifted writer, but she is also a dynamic and electrifying speaker who connects with and mesmerizes audiences by speaking from the heart and being the message that she brings. This mind-expanding book will dramatically change your life and empower you to maximize your potential by living life on your terms. Reeling from the shock waves of the tragic events of September 11th, people are beginning to ask themselves the question, "Is this all that there is to life?" Tonya answers emphatically, that there is more out there for us, we're not crazy.

I found her writing to be captivating, riveting, and life transforming. When you get to the last page, there will be a different person who closes the book, than the one who opens it. Take the time now and go to the mirror and say "goodbye" to the old you, because the gifts that you brought to the universe are about to be released and the world will be a better place because of it. Tonya you've done yourself proud.

This has been Mrs. Mamie Brown's Baby Boy,
Les Brown.

If there is light in the soul,
There will be beauty in the person.
If there is beauty in the person,
There will be harmony in the house.
If there is harmony in the house,
There will be order in the nation.
If there is order in the nation,
There will be peace in the world.
—Chinese Proverb

Life is not just about struggling to make it. We are not supposed to flutter around in darkness, hopelessly trying to find our way. A light shines in each one of us. We just have to learn how to turn it on.

I am convinced that success occurs the moment you turn your light on and decide to live the life you know you are destined to live; the moment you say, I will live a great life and do whatever it takes to make that happen. After the tragedy of September 11th, that moment came quickly for me. I realized then that true success happens the moment you light the fire of life so that it becomes the joyous, exhilarating experience it is supposed to be. For me, the fire has been lit; I turned on my light. Let the joy begin!

Tonya Kerri Johnson

SECRET ONE

DO WHAT YOU LOVE!

There is a sacred calling on each of our lives.
There is a sacred contract that you made, that I made, with
the Creator when we came into being...not just the sperm
and the egg meeting when we came into the essence of who
we were created to be. You made a contract. You had a
calling. And whether you know it or not, it is your job to find
out what that calling is and get about the business of doing
it.

—Oprah Winfrey

When you wake up everyday and go off to a job you hate, life can be hard. When you wake up everyday and go off to a job that causes you to be emotionally ill, but you are too afraid to quit because of the security of a paycheck, life will be miserable!

I know all too well about this kind of misery. I know, because I used to live a life of quiet desperation on a secure job I hated. After finishing law school, I found myself working on a job that was coveted by most attorneys. The job was prestigious on the outside, yes, but behind the doors of that law practice sat at least one bored, dissatisfied attorney doing loathsome paperwork that was endless. The saying goes, "Don't judge a book by its cover." And I say, "Don't judge a job by its title." I had a glamorously boring, well sought after position that was slowly killing me! (Did I mention I hated the job?). Someone said J-O-B really stands for Joyless Occupational Bondage, and boy was I in deep captivity!

I was stuck in a place where I never thought I would be. I had all of the material success I was "supposed" to have: a law degree from a prestigious University, licenses to practice law in not one but two states, and partnership status in a newly formed law firm. The letters "ESQ" behind my name cost me $25,000 each, but I reasoned that the money I spent on my legal education was a mere bag of shells considering all of the money I was sure to earn as a Big Time Lawyer. And the joy I would most assuredly experience from practicing law would be well worth it.

The problem was that in my heart of hearts, I was not happy. All of my life I had said I wanted to become an attorney, and then when I became an attorney, I hated it. I hated going to court. I hated legal paperwork. I hated everything about the legal system. I even hated the building where my law firm was located, the elevator, my office, my desk—everything about the place! This was not what I had imagined as the dream life of an attorney. I spent $75,000 on my law school education only to discover that I hated law. Now, that's a costly revelation!

Going to court everyday drained me. My life was a vicious cycle of working to pay the bills, paying them, then returning to work to earn more money just to pay more bills. It was the epitome of boredom, coupled with disgust, and topped off with frustration and confusion. I was just another rat in the legal rat race. I lived from Monday to Friday, counting the hours in-between nine and five, only to go home to sleep a bit before dragging myself out of bed to do the same thing all over again. This was not glamorous.

Life felt like an enormous struggle that would end in a funeral where they put me in a box as a good excuse to go off somewhere and eat chicken! What a bane existence! My creative talents were dying on the vine. I loved to write, and knew that I had a talent for public speaking. I also loved to sew, but quickly reasoned that all these skills would never pay the bills. They most certainly could not afford me the chic lifestyle that I desired. I was living exactly the life I had planned and worked for, and *I was unhappy.*

The wisdom of Joseph Campbell's words began speaking to me, "*Many people are so busy living the life they have planned, that they are not able to live the life that is waiting for them.*"

When I was eight years old, I declared that I was going to be a judge. From then on, I planned to be an attorney, and spent countless years in schools working to create the life I had affirmed. My master plan was to practice law for ten years and then become a judge. However without knowing it I had closed the door to the life that was waiting for me. But how could anyone spend $75,000 for an education and then quit? After all, *I was not a quitter.* Yet the monotony of my life was intolerable; I knew I had to do something about it. I knew that there was a fire in my belly that could not be quenched. I was hungry for more; my passion was calling me.

Pursuing my passion meant being committed to doing only that which brought me joy. The things that gave me joy were not in the courtroom. I was in love with telling stories and making people laugh! (Sometimes funny things did happen within the halls of justice, but believe me funny lawyers were not in high demand). My big issue was that law paid better and had more status. I had a lawyer's ego, so the last thing I was thinking about was doing something that brought me joy without getting a fat paycheck. I had bills to pay! Nonetheless, when money speaks louder than joy, it gives you the chance to stay miserable long enough for your motivation to kick in.

Pursuing my passion and doing what I love first meant that I had to ask the Creator to show me my purpose, put me on the path, and let me soar. I believe that if you sincerely ask God for something, you will be given an answer. The answer I received was "it is words." When this answer came to me, I was very uncertain. I asked, "Words in the Bible? Words in the library books? What words?"

It was years later before the answer to my question became clear. The first sign I received that I could actually do what I love to do, and have a sense of joy about it, was when I told my three-year old niece, Asha, a story about a fight I had in seventh grade. She practically fell out of her chair! I didn't think the story was that funny, but Asha thought it was a hoot! Her laughter gave me courage to do what I love.

At three years old, Asha persuaded me that I was a great storyteller. Sometimes, when you don't have all the answers about what to do and in which direction to go, someone will come along and show you who you are and what you need to be doing. When you hear that person's voice, believe him or her. When people tell you that you do a thing well, believe them. When people tell you that you do something so well that you could be making a mint at it, believe them and get to stepping! My niece's laughter sparked so much joy in me that I began telling more and more stories. When I received my first check for telling stories professionally—$75—I kissed the paper and thanked the Lord. I almost did not want to cash the check! It hit me, right in the middle of my indecision about my life, that this was what I was supposed to be doing. I had found my passion!

I now know that I am a communicator. I am a teacher. I am a storyteller. The funny thing is that I have been telling stories ever since I read books to my classmates in the second grade. Even when I presented evidence to a jury in the courtroom, I was telling a fascinating story. Now, I am called to use words and tell life stories in a different arena; one that will give me flexibility, the opportunity to meet all

4

kinds of people, and the freedom to look good in outfits that I make myself! Hot diggety dog!

If you have watched others living a life they love and wondered if something is "wrong" with you, consider this possibility: Nothing is wrong—nothing at all. It's quite the opposite. Things are exactly the way they should be. You are frustrated and upset with your job for a very good reason. You are ticked off with your situation for a purpose. Yup, things are just the way they should be. Why? *Because you need to be irritated enough about your life so that you will be driven to do something about it.* Dissatisfaction and anger are excellent motivation fuel. You *should* be upset with your boss, angry with your landlord, and bored with your circumstances. What else will get you to move your behind and do what makes you happy?

No, nothing is wrong with where you are, but there just may be something missing…

Consider the possibility that you can actually create a life for yourself where you love doing what you do. I now love what I do so much that there are days when I wake up and start shouting! If I can create a reality where seeing the hands of the clock strike five is no longer the most exciting part of my day, you can too! It is really possible for you to create a world in which you are happy going to work, where you wake up each morning excited about your day. Imagine actually looking forward to a Monday morning!

Let's look at your career. If you feel something is missing, figuring out exactly what it is can be difficult. Deciding what you are supposed to be doing with your life can, in fact, be very challenging. This is especially true when you have already carved out a life for yourself and everyone thinks you have "arrived." However, like me, you know better. You know there has to be more; that there is something else you should be doing with your life. You're just not clear about what that something is.

So what do you do? Find another job that will eventually bring you the same dissatisfaction? No. Changing jobs, before transforming your self-perception, will be a waste of time and you will be right back at square one. What most people do is stay on the job and become chronic complainers. Most people stay stuck. Why? Because most people don't look at how their jobs may be making them physically, as well as emotionally ill. Moreover, most people will never commit to investing the time and effort it takes to create a life filled with purpose. The truth is that leaving a job to do what you truly love takes an act of faith. Not being able to count on a steady paycheck to pay the rent is just too scary for most people. So fear will keep them where they are.

This fear quickly reminds people that doing what they really love is impossible. In the face of this fear, the security of an endless nine-to-five feels safer than chasing the uncertainty of a pipe dream. This is the point where many people resign themselves to mediocrity. They stop trying to figure out what they are supposed to be doing with their lives and begin living hours of quiet desperation, day after day, month after month, year after year. Without knowing where the time went, the job that has made them sick for their entire adult life has taken them all the way to retirement. They retire, and six months later they pass away, taking their unfinished dreams to the grave with them.

If the life you have planned is not working, it is up to you to get busy and create a new one. If the life you have designed for yourself does not fit anymore, it is time to re-design the one you have. Get busy! It is time to stir up your divine gifts so that you can live a life that fully expresses your unique and creative talents and abilities. Bless the discontent that you are feeling with your life. By blessing the

6

discontent, you are calling on yourself to do the very thing that you are predestined to do.

It is such a simple principle: *what we love to do is the very thing that we have been called to do. This is our purpose!* This is what will make each of us happy. The principle itself is simple, but I know that practicing the principle is not. Most people move from job to job and never experience the deep satisfaction that comes from doing something you love. When they get tired of job-hopping, they go back to school, obtain another degree, and then it's off to what eventually becomes another joyless job. Yet fluttering around here and there with this project, and on that job, is a waste of time; it will only make you more miserable. Secret number one to living a life you enjoy is this: Doing what we love is paramount.

When each one of us answers our divine calling (*and we all have one*), we become happier. What you love to do is not only what you have been called to do, but it is what you are *supposed* to be doing. The Creator gave you your particular gift for a reason. One way you can identify your passion is that it is whatever you would do without any thought of being paid for it. You love it so much, you do not consider it "work." Your passion is what you do with ease. If you love cooking, your passion is cooking. If you love singing, your passion is singing. If you love playing chess, it is playing chess. It is as simple, and as complicated as that.

I have a passion for storytelling. I tell stories with great love, feeling, and big energy; I love doing it! As Jack Canfield and Mark Victor Hansen write in their forward to, A 3rd Helping of Chicken Soup for the Soul, "…[Stories] awaken us from our habitual day-to-day lives, invite us to dream, and inspire us to do more and be more than we might have originally thought possible." For me, that is storytelling at its best, that is why I have such a passion for it.

Even if, in the beginning you volunteer, doing what you do out of love, the "doing" will lead you to the gold at the end of the rainbow. The mistake is to convince yourself otherwise. When I received $75 for half an hour of telling stories, I was elated. Today, earning $500 for conducting storytelling workshops almost knocks my socks off. I am living proof that you can earn money doing what you love. Who would have thought it? And even if you don't earn money for doing what you love, you will surely experience joy, abundance, and a sense of deep fulfilment; that my friend is priceless.

You and I have an advantage. We are already committed to finding our purpose. (If you were not, you would not be reading this book!). We are sincerely ready to start *doing* something about our lives. Connecting with what you love allows you to know your life's work, and find out what gives you meaning. When you know what you are called to do with your life, it puts you in a place of personal power.

How can you get clear on what your purpose is? How do you connect to what you love? Begin with the conscious intention to find your purpose. (This is a good time to pull out a notebook and pen). First, write down, *I intend to find my true purpose in life.* There it is, in black and white. Now, you are ready to create what I call a Passion List. For the next few minutes write down all of the things that you love to do, everything that makes your heart sing.

Next, think about this: What if you were told that all of your financial obligations would be met and you were free to do whatever you wanted? What would you be doing right now? How would you contribute to life? What would make you the happiest? Now write out your dream schedule and design your day. Fill it up with everything you are most passionate about, everything you love to do.

8

If you are not clear about what you love or you think you have no talent, think again, because *we all have talent.* Some people just need a little help figuring out what it is. One choice is to ask God to show you why you are here and what you are called to do. This requires patience. After you ask, be still and wait for an answer. Be open to the answer coming from a host of unlikely sources.

When you ask about living your purpose, try the affirmation prayer I used: *Dear God, Show me my purpose, put me on the path, and let me soar.* Repeat this prayer daily until you have an answer. Do not talk to people about this. This is between you and God. The answer will come. Just be patient. Expect it to come from any and all possible venues: the television, radio, children, or even a homeless person. The answers are everywhere. God shows up in all kinds of interesting ways. All you have to do is hear the answer when it comes and do not question what you hear.

Once you have heard your life's purpose and believe it, then commit yourself to it completely!

Remember, "The moment one definitely commits oneself, then divine providence moves too. All sorts of things occur to help one that would never otherwise have occurred. A whole stream of events issue from the decision, raising in one's favor all manner of unforeseen incidents and meetings and material assistance which no man could have dreamed would have come his way." —W.H. Murray

Affirmation

I am here for a very special purpose.
This day, I choose to start using my authentic gifts
and talents to their fullest.
I know that joy is my birthright
and that the Creator wants me to soar.
As God operates through me,
I am blessed and I am a blessing.
This day, I know my purpose, I am on the path, and I soar!

Prayer

Okay God.
There are certain words I have been afraid to speak.
Today, however, I am sick and tired of being sick and tired
so here they are - *I quit! I quit! I quit!*
No More! I am outta here!
I quit doing what does not give me joy.
I quit letting fear rule my life.
I quit taking up the dead space called sick and tired.
Now I will need that room
for all the blessings that are going to show up!
And even though I might be afraid,
I know that you are my source, my abundance.
As I step out of my comfort zone
I have no idea how things will turn out,
but I will do what it takes.
I trust you. With you, I cannot fail.
In the name of Jesus I pray.
Amen.

SECRET TWO

SET YOUR GOALS, LIVE YOUR DREAMS

Goals serve as a stimulus to life.
They tend to tap the deeper resources, and draw out of
life its best. Where there are no goals, neither will
there be significant accomplishments.
There will only be existence.

—Anonymous

Obstacles are those frightful things you see when you
take your eyes off your goal!

—Henry Ford

After you become clear about what you love to do, it is time to manifest your dreams. You will need small, achievable steps to take you there. Setting goals, by taking specific steps, will move you closer to your vision of living as your authentic self, and living a life you love. Setting goals is important. "The tragedy of life," Dr. Benjamin Mays once said, "does not lie in not reaching your goal, but in having no goal to reach."

So, what would you like to accomplish? Grab that notebook again and take some time to write down your answer. Living a life you love requires that you practice naming exactly what you want to do.

Why? There is no power in walking around *saying* that you want to be happy. What exactly does happiness look like

11

to you? The secret is to ask for and name the exact thing you want. If you go into the ice cream parlor and don't ask for strawberry ice cream, how will you get that particular flavor? Living powerfully also means that as you grow, you will ask for things and they will show up. You'd be surprised at how some people ask for things, and poof! They show up! You too will begin to attract the money, resources, and relationships that you need to live a life of power and purpose. You will begin to develop the power to speak things, and they will come into existence. How? God processes requests all the time. Written words, which state what you intend to do, catch God's attention as well as spoken words. When you speak with determination and conviction, and do the work it takes to make your dreams happen, you will get what you declare.

Writing your goals down will also help you articulate what you intend to experience in the future. Thoughts, which stay in our heads, are no more than fuzzy hopes and dreams—until we put them on paper. When you transfer the thought from a mere idea to paper, you turn things up a notch. You put the universe on notice. You also put yourself on notice by creating a silent contract with yourself about what you will manifest in your life. Your dream really begins when your thinking becomes activated, when you put pen to paper and set the energy into motion.

Today, it is time for you to let the universe know how serious you are. Dreamers, without written goals, are like architects without plans. Start by writing down three long-term goals, and three short-term goals. Your short-terms goals can be as short as what you want to accomplish by the end of the day, by the end of the month, or by the end of the year. Your long-term goals can be as long as what you want to complete within one to five years. Next, write down five reasons why you want to achieve each goal. Think about why you deserve to accomplish these goals. Don't worry about being profound or spiritual. So, you want to become rich and famous? Consider it a great motivating factor!

If you are blocked, or find yourself procrastinating and not writing your list of goals, sit down and ask yourself this question: Am I getting in my own way? I sure did. I would stay in my pajamas and watch Oprah when I could have been working on my career. Watching the show was good for soothing myself, but I knew I would not get this book written, nor would I be closer to living my dreams. Procrastination, of any kind, stops me from getting where I want to go. So goal number one was to stop procrastinating. I had to reprogram my mind, change those thoughts, and get my butt off the couch!

Goal setting has three stages: believing, naming, and doing. The major difference between truly successful people, and the not-so-successful ones, is that the truly successful people sincerely believe in what they set out to do. Belief, fueled with determination, will quickly put you into your powerful life. So, set your goals and then believe that you can achieve them.

"Whether you think you can, or think you can't," Henry Ford said, "you're right."

As you grow, your goals will grow and what you desire may even change. Just keep adding new goals that match the changes. The point is that all along the way, and as much as possible, you must be clear about what you want.

As you begin to believe in yourself more and do what it takes to manifest your dream, other people will begin to support you. Author John Gray said, "The world will believe in you and respond to your wishes when you first believe in yourself." Sometimes there will be moments, as you climb the ladder to your more powerful life, when other people will believe in you *even more* than you believe in yourself. When you feel like giving up on your dream, their faith will inspire you.

Your mind may rationalize, justify, or intellectualize why you cannot achieve the goals you want. You may even argue for your limitations. Let's not sabotage ourselves by giving credence to the negative chitter-chatter that limits us. I once talked myself into something that I knew was a billion-dollar idea, and within twenty minutes I talked myself right out of it! I let fear put the brakes on my idea. When fear crept in, I had to get out of my own head so I could get out of my own way. As the old African proverb says, *If there is no enemy within, the enemy outside can do us no harm.* Don't think too much. Trust your heart and your spirit, and ask the mind to follow in service to what you know is right, real, and true.

Next, name your goals. You will start convincing yourself that it really is possible to have what you say, when you hear yourself say it. You will develop your faith about your vision. As scripture teaches, faith really does come by hearing. When we are told the same things over and over again (whether they are true or not), they take root in our deepest consciousness. Repeating the truth about what you are going to do, and who you really are, also creates excitement—for others and yourself.

Every goal you name, and then diligently and persistently pursue, you will meet. If you do not meet a particular goal, something other than what you expected to happen will occur, and there is a good chance it will be even better than what you originally imagined! This is how things work in the world of persistence and dogged determination.

Everything I have ever persistently prayed for and envisioned, I have received. I have also prayed for things that didn't show up looking the way I expected, and I wanted God to take them back! They were the very things I had prayed for, yet I wanted God to take them all back and

14

quickly! That is when I learned that being clear is one of the wellsprings of our power, so I do my very best to exercise clarity at all times.

After you have written out your goals, begin reading them aloud three times a day for the next forty days. (I have come to believe that it takes forty days for the process of transformation to occur). Stating your goals aloud to yourself will plant the seeds for what you want to occur.

Let's focus for a minute on the kind of person you will have to become to reach your goal. Are you a master procrastinator? Do you need more discipline? Do you have to learn commitment so you can finish what you start? Perhaps you need to manage stress or gain greater time management skills. Exactly what kind of person do you have to become in order to do what you say you want to do? This picture of yourself is part of your vision. Let's write a vision statement to go along with your list of goals.

Vision statements, as well as goals, are very useful. Write down what kind of person you see yourself becoming. Here are examples of vision statements: I am a person who shows up on time for all of my appointments; I am a person who never sweats the small stuff. I am calm and stress free.

When you set your mind on a vision, and begin to work on it, you activate your faith. When you believe in your vision, speak it, and start working at it, it will come to pass. All of the things we want to experience start with a vision and a belief that they can happen. Having a vision is critical to our success. The scripture is clear in teaching that, where there is no vision, the people perish. The flip side of this is also true: where there is a vision, the people prosper.

When I needed to take the New York State bar examination, I practiced seeing the end result ahead of time. I imagined, in my clearest mind's eye, the suit I would wear to my swearing-in ceremony. I then made the outfit and hung it up in the closet as an act of faith. I was so sure that I would pass the bar exam that I made that new suit to show the universe that I meant business. I had to do the work, study and learn the material, and I knew I would pass. I wrote, "Tonya Curtis [my former name], Attorney-at-Law, New York State license #12345," on a piece of paper and put it above my bed. It was the first thing I saw when I woke up in the morning and the last thing I saw before I went to bed at night.

I held this vision because my goal was to pass the New York State Bar examination the very first time I took it. Failure was not in my plan. I was very clear that I would study as long and as hard as it took for me to pass. In the home stretch, I did not bathe for three days! I ate, drank, and slept the New York State bar exam. It seemed like forever for those results to come back, but come they did. And yes, I passed the New York State bar exam the first time I took it. I was an Attorney-at-Law. My goal of taking and passing the bar examination was met! The vision of me being on the roll of New York State attorneys was satisfied. On the day I was admitted, I wore the suit I made with great pride. If you work hard to get what you want and believe it will happen, the prophet Habakkuk is certainly right, the vision is yet for an appointed time. In the end it will not disappoint, it will surely come!

When Oprah Winfrey completed the Chicago marathon she said, "...There is nothing that can speak to the accomplishment that in the beginning seemed impossible." Right now, your vision may seem impossible; you may think you cannot accomplish it, but defining a vision and setting goals is the beginning of you taking charge of your destiny. And in the end, when your vision has come to pass, the feeling you will experience will be indescribably wonderful.

Affirmation

I now affirm that I am clear about my purpose in life,
and I have the strength to meet all of my goals with ease.
I trust that I am moving toward my true destiny.
I now embrace the vision of myself as the best that I can
be.

Prayer

Lord, I will live the vision of abundance that you have for
me. Lord, let me see my own potential and live the dream
you have placed in my heart. Let me speak my vision and
continue to affirm it as truth. I know You are sending me
blessings with my name on them. I pray now, Lord, that
You show me what I need to know, so that I can be the
best of the best. I am worthy of this dream, God.
Thank You, right now, for the vision and the power.
In Jesus' name I pray. Amen.

SECRET THREE

WORK YOUR PLAN

*You are searching for the magic key that will
unlock the door to the source of power,
yet you have the key in your own hands,
and you make use of it the moment you learn to control
your own thoughts.*

—Napoleon Hill

*Nothing in the world can take the place of persistence.
Talent will not; nothing is more common than
unsuccessful men with talent. Genius will not;
unrewarded genius is almost a proverb. Education will
not; the world is full of educated derelicts. Persistence
and determination alone are omnipotent. The slogan
"Press On" has solved and always will solve the
problems of the human race.*

—Calvin Coolidge

To be diligent means you are steady and earnest in your work. It also means that you are disciplined and responsible. Gary Zukav, author of <u>The Seat of the Soul</u>, says, "The difference between the life you have, and living the life you want, is *responsible choice.*" Being disciplined enough to create such a life depends upon you making responsible choices.

When you work responsibly, to develop who you are by staying focused on your intentions, you live with power. Being responsible is a choice of power. There are three things I have learned to be very responsible about—my

18

relationships, my wants, and listening to God. Of these, I consider listening to God my highest priority.

Endless possibilities exist when you are disciplined about honoring what God tells you to do. When God tells you to do something, do it. You may be pleasantly surprised by the outcome! The bible story of Jonah gives us a great lesson about listening to God.

Jonah found himself in the belly of a big fish because he did not listen to God. God told Jonah that He had a great work for him to do. He told him to go and prophesy in a city called Nineveh. This was very challenging for Jonah because Nineveh was where his enemies lived. When God told Jonah to go to Nineveh, he practically ran in the opposite direction. I can hear Jonah saying, "No. No way. Oh, no God, I am not going! Not there!"

I have been just like Jonah. If God instructed me to go left and I did not want to go, I made it clear to God that I was going right—regardless of the outcome. But if you are not disciplined about listening to the promptings of your inner voice (which for me is the Spirit of God talking), you will pay a price.

God is not a disagreeable Being. He let Jonah go in the direction he chose. Likewise, God will let us go in the direction we choose. We do not have to listen. We can choose to do exactly what we want; there is always a choice. However (HA! You knew there was a catch!), if the direction we turn towards is not the one God has suggested, we will often find ourselves in a mess, praying to God for help…just as Jonah did. Our "big fish" will be the big mess that we get into because we forgot to listen to our hearts' truth and to heed to voice of God.

Jonah jumped onto a boat, which promptly ran into a terrible storm. The sailors knew that God was after something; Jonah confessed and told them God was looking for him. They immediately threw him overboard. Jonah got swallowed up by a big fish, and had three days to think about his life and his fate. When the big fish spit him out, God told Jonah to go to Nineveh again. It was easier for Jonah to listen this time. (I wonder why!). When Jonah arrived in Nineveh, he preached and prophesied. In the end, the very same people he had feared received him well.

What's the lesson here? When we are disciplined about doing what God tells us to do, good things happen as a result. They happen even if we do not know the why or the how of things in the beginning. The truth is, we don't need specifics. What we need is a deep trust in the ultimate goodness of life, and the knowledge that God is always in control.

The Quakers have a saying, "Hands to work, hearts to God." The question now is, what work are your hands going to do? Or, are you just going to talk about what you want? Talk is cheap; it takes discipline and dedication to have a plan and make it work. So what's your plan? What do you need to get motivated and do what you have been called to do? How do you get started when you have been stuck for so long?

Well, the first thing to do is to acknowledge what you do when you feel helpless and locked in. What a lot of people do is procrastinate. Procrastination and doubt tell you that you will never be able to achieve your goals. Procrastination and doubt are insidious outgrowths of our greatest enemy, fear—the exact opposite of faith. Fear tells us that our plan cannot work. But, faith keeps us moving forward—even when we feel like giving up. Faith knows that even when everything falls apart opportunities abound, and sometimes, the best opportunity is the chance to start over again.

The key to getting motivated then is finding the blessing in our situations and moving on. Once we honor where we are, we become wiser and empowered. Try looking beyond the problem and seeing what good you can find in the experience. Think of a time when you thought you could not overcome an obstacle and you did. That took courage. That took faith. Fill your mind and spirit with that same courage and the belief that you CAN, because the truth is *you CAN succeed.*

George Bernard Shaw said, "The people who get on in this world look for the circumstances they want, and if they cannot find them, they make them." Minister Joyce Meyer says you must, "Bloom where you're planted," and I say, "You have to work your thing!"

Therefore, a major key to doing something, and doing it well, is preparation. Each one of us must get busy preparing ourselves *now* to create the *later* we dream about. Preparing yourself may mean that you have to balance your checkbook regularly, clean out the closets, or keep your mouth shut, (especially when you don't want to). Preparing also means to make yourself ready *right where you are,* and at the same time be willing to adjust your plans and surrender to God's perfect will. Prepare now, so the promises of God will come to pass later. And *later* is much sooner than we think!

Don't waste time thinking, dreaming, and talking about doing stuff, instead of actually doing it—wasting time is not an asset that leads to prosperity, that's for sure. The irony is that we waste time and do not prosper, and we do not prosper because we are wasting time. Wasting time is another by-product of fear. Re-inventing ourselves is a guaranteed magnet for fear, and it can grip us like a pit bull. Fear can also paralyze you. It leaves you unable to plan, to set goals, or to remain optimistic. But one of the best antidotes for fear is to stop focusing on the fear and start planning for the future.

So get up and get going! Dedicate this day as the day you start creating your destiny and begin working your plan. The only way to do it is to do it! Goodbye, laziness! Goodbye, couch potato syndrome! Nike is right! Just do it!

Even if you do not know how on earth your plan can work, trust that you will intuitively know. Analyze where you are right now. Then, you can decide where you want to be, and when you want to be there. Take a minute and write it down. (Again I say, we always take what is written down more seriously than ideas that float across our brain and out the front door).

Next, think about why you want to be *there,* and write that down too. This list will help you make the decisions you need to climb out of the rut. Decisions have power, and they pull one another along. When you make one small decision, it becomes easier to make the next one, and the next, and the next. Decide, and do, just one thing toward your vision each day. One step at a time, you will reach the top of your mountain. Guaranteed!

Why must you climb to your mountain to success? You are the only one who can do what you do, the way you do it. You are the only one who can work your gift with *pizzazz.* When you begin to believe, speak, and own your gifts, then you will succeed...no matter what. But, for results, you have to put your buns to work. Words have power, but actions are proof of that power. Don't tell God that you *believe,* if you are not willing to *act!*

Moreover, if you do not do what you have been called to do, the world will be at a loss. God will send someone else to do it, but no one else can do it the way you can. Expressing your unique gift is up to you and you alone.

What do you have right now that will help you manifest your dream? Go back to your Passion List and refresh your memory. You might not have a lot of money, but maybe you are bold. Boldness is an asset. For example, boldness may just be the character trait you need to meet a wealthy entrepreneur to help you obtain the funds for your next project. Are you a great speaker? Are you friendly? Think about the personality traits you possess, which ones are beneficial? There is something you have right now that will help you get to where you want to be.

So after you tap into your passion, then you need faith— faith to work the plan. Having a plan, *and faith*, makes a very strong case for your powerful life. Now it is time to go with what you've got!

I learned a valuable lesson about faith when I was in the seventh grade. For some unknown reason, the kids nicknamed me Fish-head. My clothes were a size zero. I was about five feet seven. I weighed one hundred pounds...on a good day. I was skinny skinny. At a time when the other girls were developing breasts, mine were still asleep. Once, I wore what I thought was a really hot outfit—a polka dot jumpsuit with a bodice top and bell-bottom legs—but on the day I wore it much to my dismay, I was bestowed with a new title, Fish-head in a clown suit!

As Chef Emeril Lagasse would say, my classmates sure did "kick things up a notch." (It was not a good day). In Social Studies class, a girl named Sarah kept teasing me and kicking the back of my chair. Apparently, she wanted a fight. But, I knew that if we fought, I would lose. Sarah, at two hundred pounds, scared me silly, so I kept doing my best to ignore her. This mismatch of a boxing match would be over before it began. She kicked my chair again so I started calling on my faith. Then Sarah made the ultimate mistake. She blurted out, "That's why your Mama looks like Minnie Mouse!" This was a dumb thing to say, but it was enough to set me off. No one talks about my Mama. Game over! I started formulating my plan. Fish-head was going to take care of business. I might not have had much, but I was going to go with every, skinny ounce of it!

In a split second, a new belief entered my brain. I truly believed that I could beat Sarah and win. It was a new thought for me. A new vision of myself! Oscar winner Denzel Washington said in the movie, *Fallen*, "There are moments which mark your life. Moments when time is divided into parts: before this and after this. And you know that after this, nothing will ever be the same." I was experiencing such a moment.

In that moment, I learned that in the tough times the strong people keep moving forward, no matter what they are going to find. It was a faith moment. In a split second, I moved from fear to victory; that is how faith works sometimes. In a moment, when you think you don't have it, faith sneaks up on you, and reminds you about what you *can do*. A little faith—sometimes that is all you need to get past the bumps in the road.

My faith kicked in, not to mention a little dose of insanity. I snapped. I was thinking too much. In that split second, I think I may have lost my mind. All I could think about was that Sarah was never, ever, going to talk about my Mama again. I kept telling myself that she would never talk about anybody's Mama again. And, she would definitely never call me Fish-head again. I saw the entire fight in my mind. The announcer came up to the microphone and spoke, "In this corner weighing in at two hundred pounds, Sarah, the Cow. And in this corner weighing in at a buck-o-five, (pause) Fish-head in the clown suit...Let's get ready to rumble!"

I jumped out of my chair, leaped over her desk, and pounced on Sarah like a pit bull. I thought I would beat the living stew out of her, but somewhere in the heat of battle, she started choking me. I was losing and going down for the count. Then, somehow, fate took a turn. I slipped out of her choke hold and grabbed her. Sarah accidentally hit her head against the window, and everybody thought I had done it on purpose. The kids said, "Wow, I can't believe she beat her like that: Fish-head, you got the power!" Maybe Fish-head really did have super powers (or was it just divine intervention?). Our social studies teacher broke up the fight and we both got into big trouble. But, you better believe that was the end of anyone calling me Fish-head. From then on, boldness with faith, has continued to work in my favor.

In college, I was I voted the Most Assertive and Most Influential in the senior class. I wanted to win for the Sexiest Legs, but back then my skinny chicken legs were far from sexy. Thank God my classmates saw something in me before I even knew what I was made of. As they say, everything happens for a reason.

When I wanted to meet the great motivational speaker, Leslie Calvin Brown, I had no idea how I would do it. What I did know was that since I wanted to become a professional speaker I needed a fantastic mentor. I knew I wanted to surround myself with great people and learn from only the best, and I knew the power of going for it. I wanted to work with someone at the top of the motivational food chain. That is when I knew I was voted Most Assertive and Most Influential for a pretty good reason.

So I boldly walked around affirming that Les Brown was my mentor. I even told my friends I knew him. When they asked me *how* I met Les Brown, I answered, "I haven't exactly met him yet, but that is a small detail God is working out." Why did I have such confidence? Scripture teaches that thou shalt decree a thing and it shall be added unto thee!

Furthermore, I knew that Les Brown loved sweet potato pies. I knew that he bragged about his mother and her gift of making sweet potato pies. God bless Les' mother; may she rest in peace. I am sure Maime Brown baked a pie in her day, but I know that you have not lived until you've tasted my mother's sweet potato pies! My mother's sweet potato pies will make your toes curl and have you speaking in unknown tongues!

It was no coincidence, to me, that Les Brown loved to eat sweet potato pies and my mother sure could bake 'em! That smelled like a divine connection to me! It was time to work my plan.

At that time, Les Brown worked for a radio station in New York City. He was sponsoring an event he billed as Motivational Mondays. I attended the lectures, always sat up front, and soaked in every exciting word: I was hungry for a new life. One Monday, after he spoke, I made my way through the huge crowd and handed him a bag that contained one of my mother's pies along with my business card. I said, "Mr. Brown, my name is Tonya and I know how much you love sweet potato pies. Here is my mother's sweet potato pie, and I also want you to know that it has been said that this pie will make you wanna jump up and slap your mama!" Les Brown accepted the pie with a warm, hearty laugh.

I had no doubt in my mind that he would be ready to jump out of his socks when he ate that pie. What I did not expect was the shout out, which Les Brown gave me the next morning on the radio: "This is to Tonya and her Mama for that pie—it was sho nuff!" (Which means that the pie tasted so amazing that each bite really did make him wiggle his toes and speak in unknown tongues!). Later that day, I called the radio station and told one of the staff members that I was the lady who gave Mr. Brown the pie. She told me that Les Brown did not share a single slice with anyone at the radio station. The pie was so "sho nuff," he ate the entire thing!

The next afternoon, Les Brown called me personally. Talk about excitement in my office! Usually my secretary would simply patch my calls in to me, but when she realized it was the great motivator, Les Brown, on the telephone, she jumped up out of her chair, ran into my office with arms flailing, and said, "Mr. Les Brown is on the telephone! Mr. Les Brown is on the telephone!" (This in and of itself was amazing, given the fact that my secretary was about as motivated as a paper bag. I had never seen her that lively before...or since!).

I picked up the telephone, as if Les and I had been friends for ages. "Hey Les. How you doin'?"

"Tonya," he said, "This is Leslie Calvin Brown. That pie your mother made was some kind of wonderful. I have been dreaming about your mama and that sweet potato pie!"

I excitedly said, "Thank you. I know. By the way Mr. Brown, I am a professional speaker. And I need a coach. Will you help me?"

Les Brown was more than happy to assist me. He said I had demonstrated determination and a bold spirit, and that I knew how to create my own opportunities. As Les says, *that's the stuff winners are made of.* With one "sho nuff" sweet potato pie and my bold request, I created the opportunity to work with Les as my coach.

The following week when he returned to New York, I met with Les and gave him a sample of one of my keynote addresses. Les likes to call himself the motivator, but I spoke so well that day, that I motivated the motivator! When I was done he paused before critiquing me; I was ready for him to knock me off of my motivational high horse. However, he did quite the opposite. He told me that I was a "diamond in the rough." He also said, "Tonya, I like you. You got guts!" Not a bad appraisal for someone who was just getting started, and being critiqued by one of the best in the motivational business!

Right then and there, Les chose me to become one of his personal assistants. I have had the opportunity to travel with him, sell product at his events, and to open for him. Les and I have forged a friendship, for which I am very grateful. I learned that determination, along with creative self-promotion, goes a long way! That's the meaning of my personal saying, *"Go with what you've got!"*

With Sarah and with Les, both of my lessons were about having faith—faith in what I could do, and faith in the way life would support me after I took just *one step*. And, just when you think things are not going to happen, if you have a little faith, life will turn it around for you too. Another realization was that real power comes from the choices we make. God sets up the opportunities all of the time. We just have to stand up and say, "That's it, I am going for it!" And seize the moment.

Affirmation

Today, I acknowledge that God is working things out in my favor. Today, I get up and step into a place of power by moving my buns and working my plan!

Prayer

Today, God, I stand at the door of opportunity.
I acknowledge that it is time to create a life I love.
Today, I trust the process,
even though part of me still acts afraid.
There are times when, I wonder why You chose me to do this. I feel alone and unsure.
In spite of it all, I say to You God that I will do Your will.
I promise that I will let my light shine,
so that the world may see Your excellence in me.
Even if I find myself in the wilderness,
I know You will continue to light my path with prosperity. Even if I find myself in darkness,
I know You will light my way with grace and abundance.
I know that when faith stands up, fear sits down.
Thank You. Thank You. Thank You Father, for filling me with the courage to live my dream, and go with what I've got! And so it is. In the name of Jesus I pray. Amen.

SECRET FOUR

MAINTAIN YOUR LIFE

In order to stay in order, get rid of the junk.
When you hold on to junk, it weighs down the spirit.

—Derek Keith Johnson

After you have determined your purpose and set your goals, you must maintain your life by creating order inside your physical living space. I believe that it is nearly impossible to be focused and clear about creating a powerful and purposeful life when your home is a mess. So I live by my grandmother's rule: *There is a place for everything and everything must be in its place.*

Keeping order is about taking care of your affairs, and this works best when you practice maintaining order daily. The goal here is to set priorities, keep everything in its proper place, and take care of business in advance. When you maintain order and stay organized, you stay focused and in line with your highest self.

Maintaining order in our lives comes with the added benefit of immense peace. When things are where they belong, and you know exactly where everything is, you can readily put your hands on what you need when you need it.

Putting our world in order also helps us to slow down and stop rushing. It frees up our energy so we can powerfully and purposefully move into a life that works. Ordering our hearts, minds, and surroundings, assures us that we can move up the ladder of life with ease.

Cleaning up, clearing out, and letting go is hard for some of us. But consider this, if our space is cluttered with old things, how can new things come to us? By holding on to things we rarely use, we block future blessings. If something no longer works and cannot be repaired, throw it away. I believe that people hold onto specific items because they are afraid it might be the last of its kind, but as the saying goes, "A closed hand can neither give nor receive." Begin maintaining your life by taking a powerful step to create order - give some of your stuff away.

Let me emphasize that nothing else can show up in life if you do not recycle what you do not use, or release it. You may fear giving it up, but instead of thinking about what you are giving up, why not think about what you are giving *to*? Giving is a deeply spiritual principal.

In the book of Luke, the Word teaches us to, "Give and it shall be given unto you, a good measure, pressed down, shaken together, and running over in your lap." My translation of that scripture is simple: Give and you will get even more. Don't give and you won't get!

One summer, I gave all of my furniture away. People thought I was absolutely nuts. That's okay. What I understand is that material things carry a specific energy with them. At that time, the energy of my furniture was as old and as tired as my life was feeling. It was true that I had no idea how I would buy new furniture, because my funds were tied to buying a co-op, but I gave my furniture away anyway.

Much to my surprise and delight, the spiritual law of giving fulfilled my need immediately. When I moved into my new place, the previous owner decided to leave behind a lot of his furniture. I was able to replace just what I had given away. An inner knowing prompted me to give away what I had, and I was immediately blessed with even more.

This is what happens when you let go of the fear attached to letting things go.

But why, you ask, should I clear out and clean up the clutter?

Clutter is insidious. When left unchecked, it slowly multiplies, becoming unmanageable and out of control. It starts with little piles here and little piles there, which mysteriously grow and grow and grow. They build up until they are unmanageable and overwhelming.

And if you love to shop like me, it is easy to lose control over your possessions. Therefore, whenever I buy something new, I give away something old: I refuse to get bogged down in possessions. If all I did was shop without giving anything away, a little shopping here and a little more shopping there, before you know it, I would be knee deep in clothes and clutter chaos.

No, I am not advocating that we all become neat nuts. I am speaking about not losing control, and not allowing your possessions to possess you. I am also saying to clear out long-standing junk, because there is a connection between what is happening in our lives spiritually, and what our world looks like physically. Clutter blocks the physical path and the spiritual path as well. Clutter is a spiritual block because it drains the spirit; just looking at the junk can be sickening.

Keeping things neat and clean is another one of my grandmother's rules. She has always believed in the saying, "Cleanliness is next to Godliness." Likewise, my approach to clutter management is to consider it from a spiritual point of view. That is, making a connection with what goes on inside of us, and what is happening around us. Your inside world and your outside world are interconnected.

Think about this in terms of a relationship. Over time in a relationship, a little stuff left undone (along with miscommunication) can suddenly leave you and your mate sitting in a pile of crap. You both wonder how things got so out of control, so quickly. The truth is that it did not happen "quickly." Much like physical clutter, it was unchecked, unfinished business that you both allowed to get out of control until it became so overwhelming that the only apparent choice seemed to be to close the door on the relationship. The same thing happens with clutter. It piles up and piles up, and when it becomes overwhelming, the tendency is to close the door on the mess and walk away. But by cleaning up your physical space, you also create a clearing in your life, physically and mentally, as well as give yourself the chance to gain control and re-charge your life.

There is a line from the movie, *Cry the Beloved Country,* which says, "The tragedy is not that things get broken, but that they are not put together again." A powerful person recognizes that the fault is not so much in creating the mess, but in not cleaning it up. A powerful person also knows when it is time to put things back together again and gets busy doing it.

If any of your space is a mess, unless you are a person who thrives in it, you cannot live as powerfully as you want to live. A little mess is okay, but excessive clutter has its costs. It costs us when we are scatter-brained and not able to find things. The confusion created by the clutter takes away from our time, energy, and mental health. One of the reasons you may feel stuck in your career is that you are surrounded by a lot of junk. Quite frankly, there is no way around this one; it is time to get busy cleaning.

Creating the mess took time and so will cleaning it up, so be patient with yourself. If you tackle it little by little, step by step, one day at a time, then order will come. Consider the following practical tips as *homework for the soul:*

Creating Order in the Bedroom

During one of my seminars on creating order when I asked the question, "So what's going on in the bedroom?"

Someone answered, "A hurricane!"

A hurricane. That's a mess if I've ever seen one.

Someone else answered, "Nothing, absolutely nothing!"

These responses were funny and very honest, but the real question is *why? Why has the bedroom (for so many people) become a dumping ground?* I think it is just the easiest and most comfortable room to plop down in. It is easy to take off your clothes and throw them in a pile on the floor, or on the bed (especially after a tiring day), and then plop down on the bed to fall off to sleep. However, if you are looking for a husband or wife and there is no space for him or her in your bed, the pile of clothes and all the other junk in the bedroom only adds to the problem.

There is, literally and metaphorically, no room for him or her to exist. If your soul mate did show up, where would you put this person? If there are clothes, books, and papers everywhere, something deeper is going on in the bedroom. Do you even have another pillow for your mate on the bed? Perhaps this is a subconscious way to reject the very same love, which we say we want. Maybe this happens because a part of us is not ready for the relationship. But if you want to get ready for the person, clean up and prepare a space for the dream person who you want to be dreaming with you. When you are organized in your inner space, you begin to attract what you want in your outer space.

I once had a dear friend tell me that the bedroom was for sleeping and making love to your spouse, period! He said there should be no television, no computer, or anything else in the bedroom that created a distraction. He made it clear to me that nothing should be in the bedroom but the two people, and the bed. Having grown up with the television in the bedroom, and letting it put me to sleep for many, many years, you better believe that I was not a happy camper implementing this new house rule. It took me a while to get over it, but he was right. Without a television, I slept better and the bedroom became my sanctuary.

As for other stuff in your bedroom, remember, the bedroom is not a dumping ground. It is not the place for bookshelves, computers, exercise bikes, or other workout equipment. The bedroom is not a library, office, or gym. The bedroom is the love room of your home, a place where you retreat for rest. It should be warm and cozy so you can sleep well. Additionally, if you have a television in the bedroom and refuse to part with it, turn it off before you go to sleep. Set a timer so that it will turn off automatically. This is critical because your brain processes information even when you are sleeping and there is no way you will be truly rested in the morning with the television on all night. Consider covering the television by putting a piece of cloth over it. Put it to bed also; shut down the energy.

I stopped watching the news before retiring to bed, because I found myself sleeping fitfully after listening to crime reports and the bad news of the day. Do yourself a favor and turn off the television. Listen to soft music or do some leisurely reading before you go to bed. Anything that will nourish your spirit before you retire to sleep will do.

Creating Order in Your Living Room

The living room is a place for living. It should be alive and inviting. It should not be a museum. This room is for your family and is the heart of your home. My Auntie (God bless her) kept those awful, plastic covers on her living room couch. Those slipcovers stuck to my legs in the summer. To this day, I hate plastic slipcovers. If you are tempted to buy a couch that is too beautiful for folk to sit on and enjoy, leave it in the store. My Auntie did not want anyone sitting on her couch without the plastic, and no one wanted to sit on the couch with the plastic. Very little living was going on in that living room. Who wants to be in such a sterile and cold environment? Either too clean or too messy, when a living room stops being a room for living, it is of no use to anyone.

Consider making these *little* changes, which can make a *big* difference in your living room.

- Bring in freshly cut flowers to draw people in to the room and create conversation.
- Get rid of the plastic on the furniture, so you can share the room with others.
- If people do not go into your living room, try sitting in it quietly to figure out why. What could you do to create a more people-friendly room? Maybe a fresh coat of paint? A new couch?
- Check out the lighting. Is it too dull? If possible, try increasing the wattage or adding more lamps. (Lighting will not only light up the space, but it will "lighten up" the environment).
- Put up artwork with people laughing and having a good time.

Creating Order in Your Bathroom

Bathrooms are where you refresh and renew. Personally, I think a lot of people have a hard time releasing physical and mental stuff because their bathrooms are a mess. I wouldn't be surprised if people who live with very messy bathrooms, or overly clean bathrooms (either extreme is troublesome) have problems with digestion or their colon. Remember whatever happens with you internally is reflected externally in your environment.

A friend once told me about a woman who had a picture in her bathroom of a couple straining while pulling on the American flag. Was it any surprise that this woman was always constipated? Bathrooms need to be one place where nothing blocks your path physically or spiritually. Bathrooms should be a place where you are at ease. If you are like me, you spend a lot of time thinking in your bathroom, so order is essential for clarity.

Consider making the following changes in the bathroom:

- Keep magazines in your bathroom *current*.
- Be sure all the pipes and drains are free flowing with no leaks.
- Have your bathroom well lit.
- Change your shower curtain liner when it gets old.
- Always keep the area under the sink neat and clean.
- Keep the mirrors clean.
- Add fresh flowers, or a beautiful, healthy plant.

Creating Order in the Closets

Closets are where we store clothes and various items. Closets are not hideaway spots for junk. So, what do your closets look like? (If you need to put the book down for a minute and take a breath here, that's okay). I know closets are easy hiding places—just push the stuff in and no one will ever see it. But *you* always know what is going on behind that door. The stuff in your closet, that no one sees, might represent all the secrets that you are hiding, or issues you want to ignore. Take a look at what you refuse to deal with. Why has this mess been in there for so long?

All of our external "stuff," and what we do with it, is so much more than just a pile of physical belongings that we are hiding away. What is it that you do not want to let go of? Is it a person? A memory of something? An issue? Think about it. Closets may take a while for you to get around to dealing with, but just do it—no matter how long it takes. You have my support.

And even if your closets are neat, it won't hurt to reorganize them. How about putting all of your clothes on fancy, matching hangers to give the closet a more organized look? If your closet is neatly filled with old clothes that you have been meaning to give away, now is the time to give them away. Clean out the clothes that you no longer use, for whatever reason. They have no business being in a bag at the bottom of your closet.

Why hold onto old clothes, which no longer fit you and you have no plans to wear? If your issue is losing weight, and the goal is to get into those clothes again, give yourself six months. If you lose the weight and can fit back into those clothes, wonderful! If not, give them away! If you do keep those clothes, by the time you get back to the size you want, they may be so outdated that you wouldn't wear them anyway.

I am not suggesting that you give away all of your clothing. If something has sentimental value, by all means keep it. However, whatever you don't use (and probably never will) is what has to go. Give it up, give it away, or discard it, and trust that someone else will put to use what you not longer need. Meanwhile, because you have plenty of living to do, you are freed of stuff and ready to soar.

Creating Order in Your Kitchen

The kitchen is, quite literally, where love is designed. Preparing and sharing food is a powerful act of love that deserves a clean environment with upbeat vibrations, and a person cooking must have a healthy attitude. Food tastes better when you cook it with love. My rule of thumb is to stay away from the kitchen when you are upset or having a heated argument. Why? I believe that the heat from cooking can spill over into your emotional pot, adding to the fire of an argument. If you can't cook when you are happy, don't bother cooking at all; an upset attitude will upset the entire meal. Heat a frozen dinner instead.

Creating Order with Your Money

Money needs to be taken care of. This is how the rich get richer—they take care of their money. They value their money. I don't mean worship money. Money is not God. Money is money, and it needs to be taken care of. Money is as good, or as bad, as we feel about it.

When you value money, it means you respect it by taking care of your finances. All money, from one penny to millions, must be taken care of. For example, when you have crumpled up dollar bills scattered throughout your belongings, it shows a lack of care. The rich know how to care about money. That's how they became rich in the first place. They master the art of taking care of all of their money, even the smallest amounts. They understand the saying, "Take care of your money, and your money will take care of you."

Mega-millionaire, Donald Trump, says, "Fight for the pennies, and the dollars will come." So stop and pick up the pennies when you see them. Consider them "pennies from heaven." When I see pennies, I am reminded of God's promise of abundance for me. The more pennies I find, the happier I get. Take care of precious penny and mama dollar will smile upon you!

A good place to start taking care of your money is by cleaning out your wallet or purse. Suze Orman, author of the bestselling book, _The Nine Steps to Financial Freedom_, advocates that a pocketbook or wallet should be kept orderly at all times. Your success for attracting money will happen when you respect what you already have. Let's get started today. Put the book down, take a minute now, and clean your wallet or purse (if you need to).

Be careful not to accumulate paper clutter also. Paper clutter can block the flow of money. How so you ask? Dollars are made of paper. Dollars are currency and currency by definition, must circulate. I believe that on the spiritual level, dollars have a difficult time moving when pounds of paper are in their way. Paper clutter can block the flow of currency in the physical realm.

My direct experience with this occurred when I was a partner in my law firm, I remember desperately waiting for an $8,000 check from the agency I was doing work for. The more I waited, the longer it took for the money to come. I prayed for the check and was even told that it was in the mail, but two weeks after my request, I still did not have the money. If I didn't know better, I would have thought that they were sending the money by a mule! The office rent was late, the staff needed to be paid, and the telephone company was about to disconnect my phone – I was in a financial hot pot that was getting hotter by the minute!

That is when I looked at my desk and it hit me! I had a stack of legal work so high it should have been a crime. Those legal papers I was too lazy to deal with were holding up progress on my client's cases. I wasn't receiving an important piece of paper (in this case the check) because I wasn't giving away any important papers. In that moment, my new Friday evening plan was to stay after work and clean up that pile no matter how long it took. Six long hours later, I was done. With all of the legal motions complete, and the documentation done, I finally felt I could rest. Not by coincidence, the following Wednesday, I got a call to come and pick up the $8,000 check!

Creating Order with your Artwork and Home Decor

Every item that decorates your home reflects something about you. When you pay attention to each thing that is around you, you are in effect paying attention to yourself.

A good example of this is mirrors. Each time you look in a mirror, the reflection smiling back should be clean and clear. This external reality corresponds to the internal image of yourself that needs to be uncloudy and unmistakable. Cracked, cloudy, or dusty mirrors cannot reflect the you who is living a powerful and purposeful life. If you have mirrors in your home, I implore you to keep them clean, and if they are broken or cracked, replace them immediately. Imperfect mirrors suggest a fractured, cracked, unclear, and warped image of YOU. I don't even like sectional mirrors because they create a split "you" who is divided into sections. I believe looking at yourself in this way may amount to frequent indecision, which is not a state of power. As you begin to take steps towards empowering yourself, you will be amazed at how much of a difference keeping your mirrors clean will make.

Like mirrors, the artwork you choose also makes a statement about you. When I went through my girlfriend's home, we took a good look at her artwork. Most of it was reflected around themes of fear and despair. This was not surprising. At the time she purchased these paintings, she was in an abusive marriage where she felt desperate and helpless. One painting, near her front door, showed slaves trying to escape, with Harriet Tubman holding a gun. Not only was this painting beside the front door, but the gun was pointed directly at whomever entered her home. "Not too many people coming over lately?" I quipped.

Walk through your home and look carefully at all of your artwork. Ask yourself, what does this piece say to me? What feelings does it bring up? What was I experiencing when I bought it? How did I feel when I purchased it? Do I feel the same about it now? Does a particular part of my body hurt when I look at it? When I come near it, does my body want to move closer, or away from this piece? If you have artwork that you bought during a dark period in your life, seriously consider letting it go.

Also, be sure to update old photographs of friends, family, and yourself. Even if you keep the older photos for a historical time line, continue to add current ones. And check out your driver license photo, and your employee identification picture. Do they still look like you? Have you seen some of the pictures that people have on these identification cards lately? The picture looks nothing like the actual person, especially if he or she has gone through any major life transformation. I have changed my driver's license photo three times in three years, not worrying about the eight dollars it cost each time to change the photo, or how much I might be annoying the Department of Motor Vehicle photographer. A good picture of myself was well worth it!

Remember, maintaining order in your life takes time. Assess what you have to do and keep at it, one step at a time. Don't rush yourself. And don't be hard on yourself during the process. It took time for things to fall out of order, and it will take time to pull them back together. When you establish order, even with just a few small things, you are well on your way to living a life you love.

Affirmation

Today, I ground myself in the principle of order.
I begin to stand in my own power.
I know that things will be turned upside-down
before I create the order I seek;
it is always darkest before the dawn.
I must go through before I come out.
This is the nature of getting my life in order.
I have faith that, with God, my steps are ordered, and
that I will remain strong and disciplined while I clean
up and clear out. By creating order in my life, I create a
life of purpose and power.

Prayer

Dear God,
Today I seek order. Today I will clean up.
Today I choose to let go and give up those things
I no longer use, need, or want.
Today I am in order. In the name of Jesus. Amen.

SECRET FIVE

CHOOSE PEACE

We can say 'Peace on Earth',
we can sing about it, preach about it, or pray about it,
but if we have not internalized the mythology
to make it happen inside of us, then it will not be.

—The late, Dr. Betty Shabazz

"That the birds of worry and care fly over your head,
this you cannot change, but that they build nests in your
hair, this you can prevent."

—Chinese proverb

Living in peace is a conscious choice, which is essential to self-preservation. I often say that if I have to choose between someone being upset with me, or my own peace of mind, there is no question which one I will choose. I have made a decision to put personal peace at the top of my list of priorities.

I believe that the people who do not choose to live in peace can often be stricken with an affliction that the old folk call "worriation." I define "worriation" as engaging in the act of worry on such a consistent basis and in such a persistent manner, that it becomes life threatening or even fatal.

If you must choose between your own peace of mind and making someone else happy, there should be no question about which one to pick: Make yourself happy; dump the drama! No, you are not being selfish. You are engaging in a critical act of self-preservation. You are meeting your goal of living in total peace. My cousin Ozzie has a saying: "I don't do drama and I don't do stress." This is how I choose to live and this is how you must choose to live for serenity's sake.

Choosing the kind of life where you live in peace necessitates that you keep away from negative people who do not support your decision to live better. My mentor and friend Les Brown says, "Seek out those people who empower you, who inspire and compliment you, the people who enable you to see great possibilities for yourself. It takes an enormous amount of energy to reach your goals and to strive continuously for greatness. You really cannot afford to have relationships with people whose very presence drains energy from you."

Many people do not achieve their goals because they never move away from the negative people around them. Negative people are dead weight. Running with negative people is like trying to run a marathon with a brick tied around your neck; they will bring you down every time.

I have often wondered why people spend so much time and energy in relationships that do not honor who they are. Perhaps the contentment and complacency of what is familiar is easier than the uncertainty of the unknown, but I agree with George Washington Carver when he said, "It's better to be alone than to be in bad company." Or, perhaps, some people are so worried about hurting other people's feelings, and not burning the bridge that connects them to those folk, that they hang on in spite of the negative relationship. Let's be clear, leaving a situation where you are no longer respected or honored, or where you are being treated badly, is not burning a bridge; it's taking care of yourself. It is an act of self-preservation and love. It is futile to worry about what someone will say, or if they will be angry with you when you finally decide to leave. Stop wasting your energy.

Some of us use all kinds of excuses to stay stuck in toxic relationships, but behind this smoke screen lies the real issue: We have a hard time believing that there will be other people who will show up and give us exactly what we need, when we need it. We forget that the people, who can help us on the road to our dreams, are not in limited supply.

One of my spiritual teachers, Nancy, once asked me this question when I refused to leave a bad relationship. She said, "What's the mark on your soul? What's the price for hanging out with this person? What are you becoming as a result? What's the price you are paying?" She also said that I was a bird with clipped wings, and instead of flying high I was living low. I hated hearing it, but it was the truth. The stress of staying in a negative, toxic relationship taxed my peace of mind and my well being.

We don't move forward into a powerful life by staying in relationships with negative people. As they say, "Birds of a feather, flock together." When you hang out with negative people, you become negative. You pick up their negative acts, their negative habits, and most of all, their negative ways of thinking about life.

When assessing a relationship, ask yourself if the relationship is helping you to become a better person. If not, it is time to make new choices. Choosing to let toxic people go (no matter who they are in our circle of friends) is well worth it in the long run. It makes no sense to read empowerment books, attend all kinds of motivational workshops, and then keep hanging out with tired, toxic, ugly people.

And don't play yourself cheap! In 1994, in his inaugural address, President Nelson Mandela quoted author and spiritual teacher Marianne Williamson when he said, "You are a child of God and your playing small does not serve the universe. You were born to make manifest the glory of God that is within you." You are indeed a child of the Most High God. Live in the glory of that reality. Leave the negative folk alone. Do yourself a favor and foster new relationships with only positive people. Positive relationships provide you with the best support you need to fly to your greatest potential.

Affirmation

I surround myself with loving, positive people who continue to support my growth and development.

Prayer

Dear God:
I know that there is a better way. With Your help, I will no longer remain in situations that do not serve me. I will no longer stay in places where I am not expressing my true creativity. With Your grace, I am able to move into places and relationships where I grow and experience abundance.
In the precious name of Jesus, I pray. Amen.

SECRET SIX

LIVE IN INTEGRITY
& TRUST YOUR FEELINGS

The truth shall make you free.

—John 8:32

If you want to live more powerfully and step up to a life you love, you must be honest with yourself about your life. Start by telling yourself the truth. Admit that the situation is what it is, and you created it. Guess what else? Your life is what it is, and you now have the power to fix it. It is what it is, and God still loves you. Yesterday you may have done things that were contrary to your greatness as an individual. Today, you do not have to do those things anymore. Today, you can begin to live in integrity.

We live in integrity by living whole, not perfect, just whole. We live in integrity when we decide to pick up the pieces, close out all of the unresolved issues, and clean up all of the unfinished business.

For a long time, I ignored my problems. Oddly enough, I thought they would just go away. However, the beauty of seeking to live in integrity is that it will cause you to desire to live in such a way that you can no longer deny what you feel and you can no longer ignore the truth about your life. That's precisely why I took action.

I took back my integrity when I stopped living a life of false pretenses. I had to stop lying about who I was and stop pretending about what I wanted to become. For example, I stopped pretending that my career was working when I knew good and well I hated it. In the area of my finances, I stopped pretending that I could afford things when I did not even have five hundred dollars in the bank. I also stopped spending the rent money on expensive shoes I did not need, and finally decided to pay my debts first before purchasing another unnecessary thing. I even stopped the process of buying a home because I first wanted to pay back the people I owed money to before taking on the responsibility of home ownership. After doing all of these things, that is when I started living in integrity.

I continued to live in integrity when I realized that in my relationship, little problems that bothered me about the person were really big problems that would never go away. I could no longer ignore an important relationship integrity rule: What you see is what you get. Maya Angelou said it best, "When people show you who they are, believe them the first time!"

In relationships, you operate from a place of power and integrity when you understand this rule. It is not what you THINK you see, what you WANT to see, what you HOPE to see. It is not what you THINK you might see after you have prayed hard enough, or what you think you might see after aimlessly spending too much money talking on the psychic hotline. But it is this: WHAT YOU SEE IS WHAT YOU GET! *Listen to your first mind.* If you see a man who has five kids and is not taking care of them, he is a man who will not take care of your children. If you see a woman who is abusive to her father (or mother), she will be abusive to you. If you see someone who is loud, drunk, and dirty, that is what that person is. A person can change, but just because he or she gets hooked up with *you* does not mean that he or she *will* change. Therefore, don't forget the basic truth about living in integrity: *Always trust your feelings and follow your first mind.*

If you try to make a relationship work by attempting to make the person something other than what they are, unless he or she is willing to change, that person will remain the same. What you see in the beginning is what you will painfully experience in the end. Don't make the mistake I made of staying in a relationship *hoping* that the person will change. We don't date, romance, or marry a hope; we get what is.

Sure, in life, people improve and change for the better; however, some things are so intrinsic to a person's character that change on a soul level might take two lifetimes to occur. You are not God, Jr. If you cannot accept people for who they are right where they are, leave them alone. If you don't leave them alone, and you know that you should, you will experience the pain that comes with ignoring the principle of what you see is what you get. To put it another way, there is an old saying, "What the ears don't hear, the behind will feel!" Trust me, I know what I am talking about. Because I did not listen to my ex-husband when he said, "I just don't think I am ready for marriage," I now know the pain of divorce.

The truth is that I still have a hard time with trusting myself completely and telling myself the truth; I admit it is a challenge for a lot of us. Sometimes, I wonder if it is the voice of God I hear telling me to move forward or to stop and be still, or if is my own desire getting in the way. My advice is that when unclear about what to do, be still and focus. Be still so that you can hear your heart. When you can't sit still long enough to hear your inner voice, you will get lost in the drama of your own agenda. Be still and learn to trust what you feel so that you can make choices that will honor you as you start living in integrity.

Here is a another homework assignment for you: Use a watch with a second hand, or get a timer, and take five minutes to be with yourself before the end of this day. (Just five minutes out of a whole day!). Go to a quiet, comfortable place where you will not be interrupted. Turn off the ringer or unplug the telephone. Turn off the cell phone and leave the television off as well. This is important. If someone calls you and you miss the call, that person will call back if it is important.

Rest your mind. Ask your heart what you should do about your life affairs and your relationships. Trust whatever you begin to feel. Check in with what your heart feels, and do not ignore it. Start affirming that you trust yourself now and always. Tell yourself that you will be and always are divinely protected and loved in all of your relationships. Start with this little step. This is a process. Continuously remind yourself that you now choose to honor and acknowledge what you feel when you feel it. Do it, and you begin to live in integrity.

Affirmation

I will live as a vessel for truth.
I will live consciously.
I will live in integrity by doing exactly what I say I will
do. I will live in a space where I handle all of my
financial affairs and my relationships. I hear and follow
the voice of God. I will listen to my heart the first time.
I will live whole. I will live in integrity.

Prayer

Dear God:
Let my light shine as I live in the world.
Let me live each day honoring my word in all things.
Let my light shine as I honor who I am.
Let me live each day in service to You.
Let me live with integrity.
In the name of Jesus. Amen.

SECRET SEVEN

WATCH YOUR WORDS

Death and life are in the power of the tongue.

—Proverbs 18:21

Words have power. Thoughts have power. Thoughts have energy. You can make or break your world by your thinking.

—Susan Taylor
Publication Director
Essence Magazine

In his book, *The Four Agreements*, Don Miguel Ruiz says that we must be impeccable with our word. He writes, "Your word is the gift that comes directly from God. Through the word you express your creative power. It is through the word that you manifest everything... The word is not just a sound or a written symbol. The word is a force...the word is so powerful that one word can change or destroy..."

Your word is powerful—very powerful. Your word can truly harm or destroy. One small word you speak can cause a lot of pain or bring a lot of joy. Most people do not pay close attention to the power of their words, or how their words ring with a specific energy. When two people say the very same thing, but one uses a loving spirit and gentle tone while the other person speaks with a nasty attitude, who do you think will get the better response?

Before preaching, I have heard some pastors say, "May the words of my mouth and the meditations of my heart be acceptable in thy sight, oh Lord, my Strength and my Redeemer." They knew that when we speak, we create a sacred contract with ourselves, and the person with whom we are speaking. A good rule to follow therefore is, think before you speak. If you do not know what to say, do not speak.

The sacred contract we create when we speak means we must honor our word. We all need to be what I call *"count-on-able."* If you want to count on people, be sure they can count on you. Be consistent with what you say and do. If you say you will be somewhere, show up! If you say something, and you cannot do it, renegotiate what you said. If you do not renegotiate your word and dishonor your agreement, you will feel the pain of not living in agreement with your words. The pain of not living in agreement with your words is felt when people begin to say you are unreliable or begin to believe you really are untrustworthy. That is a hurting feeling. Always honor your word.

That sacred contract also states that we must watch our mouths. When children find the nerve to talk back to us, the first thing we say is, "Watch your mouth." We warn them that their words will get them into big trouble if they are not careful. What we are teaching them is the principle of standing guard over their mouths. After we tell our kids this, it is a good idea to remind ourselves of this sacred principle as well. Literally speaking, big mouths can get into trouble every bit as much as little mouths.

I remember a lesson I learned about talking too much. When I was young, my mother was washing my sister's cloth diapers; I stood there sassing her because she would not let me do things my way. (I was pretty good at being a smart mouth when I got going). Mom kept telling me, "Watch your mouth. Watch your mouth." But I was not hearing a word she said. I have no idea where I got the courage to talk back, but I knew I was going to have to pay for it sooner or later.

My sooner came much quicker than later when all of a sudden my mother took that wet diaper and popped me right in the mouth with it! My mother did not miss a beat; she went right on back to washing those diapers as if nothing happened. My lips burned and my cheeks ached, but I sure learned the lesson of watching my words. I did not renegotiate those words and Lord knows I felt the pain because of it. I also learned how and when to shut up.

I really learned to honor this principle one summer after running around telling everybody my issues, asking for other people's opinions and insights. (I temporarily forgot about the principle of shut-up-ness). Finally, my spiritual mother told me to stop telling everybody everything, and to stop listening to their responses. She said, "Tonya, you cannot listen to other people. They do not know their own way; how can they possibly tell you which way to turn, where to go, and what to do?" She reminded me I was going to do it the way I wanted to anyway, so why not follow my own voice and the direction of God?

Another aspect of the sacred contract is to always be mindful about what you say about yourself to yourself. If you find yourself engaging in a negative conversation in your head say, "I cancel this thought." Don't allow your own words to dis-empower you. Keep your thoughts pure, wholesome, and clear. Be careful what you say about who you are and what you want. Speak with clarity and conviction about yourself.

Try, for the next hour, to speak only that which is positive. Do not gossip about your personal business, or anyone else's. Do not utter a negative word about yourself or your circumstances. Do not use the words, "never" or "can't." This language limits us. Start with one hour. Start looking at, and carefully examining, your words before you speak them. Be conscious and careful of what you say. When you start to say something you do not mean, be honest and say what you do mean. Recognize when you are using language that could limit yourself and others.

Then tomorrow, make a conscious choice and do not speak negatively for half the day or the entire day if you can. If you find yourself using self-defeating language, such as, "I would do it but," or "I can't do it because," refrain from speaking this way. When you feel as if you want to utter something negative, catch yourself. If you do say something that is not powerful, cancel the words. Remember, say out loud, "I take it back. I cancel that." Do this before the words take hold in the universe.

Allow one day to become three days, and then one week. This is how good actions become great habits. This will keep you on the path to always watching what you say and checking yourself when your words are out of alignment with who you want to become. It will also allow you to begin the transformation process into a very powerful human being.

Finally, when choosing your words, keep in mind that the words you choose today will impact your tomorrows. As the saying goes, *what goes around comes around.* When I was five, I talked about my Aunt Lucy. Back then, I thought Aunt Lucy was the weirdest person on the planet. She had a hundred plants in her tiny home, slept with her teeth in a cup, and had a funny-looking husband with a shiny, bald head. My mom told me that one day I walked into Aunt Lucy's home and criticized everything in sight. I said her house looked like a jungle with all those plants in it, and that her husband reminded me of uncle Fester on the Addams Family! (Lord only knows what would have come out of my mouth if I had seen her teeth in the cup!). Guess what though? Thirty some years later, I have more plants in my home than you can imagine. I lost my front tooth so I have to sleep with my tooth in a cup until I get an implant, and my ex-husband was going bald. Watch your words!

Affirmation

I know there is power in my spoken word.
So, this day, I practice ordering my thoughts
and guarding my tongue.
I know when to talk, when to listen,
and when to practice the art of shutting up.
If I am unclear about what to say,
I choose to breathe before I speak,
clear my mind, center myself, and
make sure that my words are acceptable
in the eyes of the Creator.

Prayer

Dear God:
In the past, I have broken promises and said "Yes"
when I meant "No." I have also said "No" when I meant
"Yes." With your help, I will now honor all of my
words. I will be clear about the power of my spoken
word. I will always think and pray before I speak. I pray
this prayer in the name of Jesus. Amen.

SECRET EIGHT

MAKE IT OKAY TO CHANGE

Lord make me so uncomfortable that
I will do the very thing I fear.

—Actress Ruby Dee

Get out of the rut you are in,
and shake off the buggah-wuggah.

—Brenda Crocker

Have you ever felt like you've been left with your tail hanging in the wind after a relationship, a new idea, or a new job did not work out? After all of your hard work and efforts fell through, were you just standing there looking silly and feeling hurt? I certainly have had that experience.

The good news is that things may not have worked out this time, but sometimes not getting what you want is a blessing in disguise. Life always has a Plan B when plan A fails. Plan B says, *it is okay to begin again.* Inside of Plan B lies your flexibility and your bounce back power. Plan B says, worse things could be happening than just being left with your tail hanging in the wind. Plan B understands that today's failure can put you on the path to tomorrow's fortune. Plan B lets you know that it is more than okay, that it is perfect for you to begin again.

Susan Taylor, the former Editor-in-Chief of Essence magazine said, "We bring about new beginnings by deciding

58

to bring about endings. To renew your life, you must be willing to change, to make an effort to leave behind the things that compromise your wholeness. The universe rushes to support you whenever you attempt to take a step forward. Any time you seek to be in harmony with life, to make yourself feel more whole, all the blessings that flow from God stream toward you to bolster you and encourage you..."

About two years ago, I was faced with implementing Plan B. My gut told me that it was time to leave my law firm, yet it was one of the hardest decisions I have ever had to make. I was the one who introduced the Senior Partner—the former Commissioner of the New York City Department of Corrections—to the other partners, and now I was going to leave.

I had the boldness to court my Senior Partner, who had the $50,000 needed to start a law firm, when I did not even have $50 in the bank. And it all happened when I mistook her for a client at an administrative hearing. After a profuse apology, she and I hit it off. Between my drive and ambition, her money and amazingly good heart—and a lot of hard work—the law firm of McMickens, Curtis, Ellis, and Moore opened. [My last name was Curtis at the time].

Even then, I knew that I did not want to practice law forever. When the junior partner left the firm, my sister constantly teased me saying, "McMickens, Curtis, Ellis, and NOOOOO Moore!" While my sister laughed at me, I wrestled with how to tell my partners that I wanted to leave as well. During that time, I affirmed that I was a happy, powerful speaker and professional children's storyteller. In my heart, I knew I wanted to be a regular on Sesame Street, and that idea made me very excited. But the fear of leaving my law firm outweighed the excitement of change. Juggling with the decision was worse than making the decision itself; indecision was driving me crazy.

After months of struggling with indecision, I decided I had enough. Yes, my decision to leave came on the heels of another partner's departure and I felt awful, but I still I had to end the partnership. That's when my ego taunted me: my name would vanish from the partnership wall, no more trial excitement, no more winning satisfaction at the great oratorical contest called court. I had to quiet the ego that loved title and status, and all the perks (like having my own personal secretary). Somehow, eventually, I was able to leave in peace.

A month later, when I let go, moved forward, and accepted the change, I found myself at a conference with a Sesame Street cast member. This was not a coincidence. Someone once said coincidence is just God's way of staying anonymous. I took it as confirmation that leaving the law firm was the right thing to do. After the conference, I was invited to a tour of the Sesame Street set. As I talked to people on the set, I could see myself doing just what I had claimed I would do, perform children's stories on Sesame Street. If I had not been willing to change, and leave my law firm when I felt something pulling at my heartstrings, I may never have had that Sesame Street opportunity.

But how do you know when it's time to change?

When things no longer work, when people no longer serve you, or when you no longer serve people, it is time to change. It is time to change when all you are doing is spinning your wheels in one place. Make no mistake—change can be frightening. But not changing can cost you everything! I think some people don't change because they are afraid—afraid of what people will say, afraid of how things will look out of their comfort zones, afraid of success…afraid, afraid, afraid. But when you feel the yearning to move, you must. Trust that change will be good, that divine opportunity is just around the corner.

My mother always says, "Sometimes, in order to get something, you have to be willing to give something up." Change keeps us growing and becoming the best we can be. If only a quiet whisper of you feels the need to change, know that life supports that part of you.

I realize that endings are frightening and new beginnings are often difficult, but in order to obtain new results, we must do new and different things. Changes and challenges are an integral part of our process toward success. Each experience has put you exactly where you need to be right now. Each experience that ends is but the beginning of where you are going to be.

Think about your dreams and aspirations. What is it you really desire? What do you want to happen? If your life were rich in every area, what would it look like? What would change? Take some time and think about this. Dream about the things you would change, if you could. Dreams give birth to visions, and visions become your reality, if you are willing to work for the changes. What can you start doing today to work on your dream?

Re-defining your life, taking control of your destiny, requires that you grab hold of your circumstances and re-create things. What small, single step forward can you take today to work on your dream? Every day you can move closer towards your goals. Each day is a wonderful day to begin again. Each day presents new opportunities and chances for us to make better choices. Change is okay!

So, where do you start to change? With yourself! To really change, you have to look in the mirror and do a self-check. Take a close look at what you have done and are doing—not what the "other" person is or isn't doing. This is not about anyone else but you.

Checking ourselves is about taking responsibility for our own actions, feeling the pain of what we have created, and dealing with it. It necessitates that we stop casting blame and become morally answerable for our "stuff." It is taking a look in the mirror and making a choice to accept the truth of our own actions.

Too often we blame other people for how we feel and what we do. Because nobody wants to be the bad guy, sometimes we conveniently forget when it is our fault. We get lost in finding fault within everyone else. But how about doing a self-check? How about doing a little self-examination? How about changing what you *believe* to be true into what *really is true*? Instead of becoming annoyed with the other person, consider the fact that if we are annoyed by our brother's actions, we are actually annoyed with ourselves.

The next time you are ticked off with someone, stop! Make a change and ask, *what is it, exactly, that is annoying me?* Take a good hard look. Then ask, *how am I like that?* You will probably resist thinking that your boss (who may be making your life a living nightmare) actually mirrors something in you. You may not intentionally inflict emotional distress on people, as he or she does, but what part of you does your boss reflect? Are you controlling? Do you rule your domain with an iron fist? Are you bossy sometimes? Are you short with people? Are you irritable, or too sensitive? The anger in your boss may mirror your own in some way and it may be something you need to change. Even if it is only a small part of you, this is where you need to focus and change. No, your boss will not magically change once you change yourself. But when his or her actions no longer trouble you, you will respond to him or her differently, and create new possibilities for the relationship.

When I do a self-check, and make a choice to change, the real learning lies in the fact that I am not just my brother or sister's keeper, but that I am my brother and my sister. The Aborigines of Australia say that, "self and others are one." Whatever is wrong with "them," needs to be made right within us first. Everything that irritates us, plucks our nerves, and upsets us about others, will lead us to a truth about how we irritate and upset ourselves. Accepting this truth is the first step towards being accountable for our actions and changing our reality. When your reality shifts, you will no longer be consumed by what others do, because you will keep the focus on what you are doing. When you are different, people respond to you in a different way.

Who is it that annoys you the most in your life? Who really gets under your skin? Write down this person's name. Make a list of the top five things that annoy you most about this person. Look at the list. Is there anything on your list that could describe you? (Be honest here).

Whatever we need to work on and change is always right in our faces.

In a previous relationship, I sat down and made a list of what perturbed me most about my mate and how that reflected me. Here's the list: I felt he ate too fast. I felt he was getting fat. I felt he did not honor his body by exercising and he was a people pleaser—too nicey-nicey. I also felt he was getting old too fast and that he did not take time out to enjoy life.

Guess what? You got it. All those things were *exactly* what bugged me about myself: I did not eat well. I did not take care of my body. I worried too much about what people thought of me. I also feared getting old. I was not living a full, rich life. And all the while, as I was complaining and moaning about what my mate should have been doing to make me happy, life was passing me by.

If your life is passing you by, it is never too late to start anew. There's nothing to lose...except maybe all the heartache caused by the regret of not changing what you could change. Keep the faith as you change. It really is possible to live a life you love.

Affirmation

Today, I commit to change-
to seeing problems as divine opportunities.
I will change my thoughts and my words.
I see change as a time to grow, a great time to heal.
I will change whatever no longer serves my life.
Today, I choose to see the good in each experience.
I give thanks for change; it allows me to step into my
destiny and live a full, rich life. In my heart, I am
willing to change and put my hands to work. When
opportunity knocks, I will be focused, ready, and able.
I commit to change.

Prayer

God, I need to change quite a few things
because my life, as it is, is just not working.
And I know God that you will respond to the smallest
invitation. So here it is: "HELP!"
Help me change my attitude about my own
circumstances, Help me remember that you continue to
work on my divine plan and order my steps. Help me
change what I can and accept what I cannot. Help me
change with ease. In Jesus' name. Amen.

SECRET NINE

CREATE YOUR JOY

I celebrate myself, and sing myself.

—Walt Whitman

*Joy comes from self-acceptance, compassion for others
and understanding that we are not the center of the
universe. It expands within us as we become
acquainted with our purpose and follow our path. It
lights up others when we love them for who they are,
not for what we wish they would become.
When we are thankful for what we have,
our joy soars, for gratitude is the mother of joy.*

—Loretta LaRoche

Enjoy a Moment of Solitude

If you are not feeling joyful, now is probably a good time to renew your spirit. Experiencing solitude is a good way to do that. Go within and revive yourself - no television, no radio, no telephone, just you and God. Sometimes, we need to clean the cobwebs out of our minds in order to re-establish joy. In the quiet times, we can connect with God and celebrate who we are.

When I took a moment for myself, I became thankful for who I am. I looked at myself in the mirror. I mean, really looked at myself and I smiled. I smiled because, even though I had been through some difficult times, I made it! With

God's help I made it through heartaches, difficulties, temporary financial setbacks, and a whole host of sticky, icky issues. I celebrated and found the joy of just being with myself. I looked at myself in the mirror, and for the first time in a long time, I liked the person I saw.

At the end of the day, when it is all said and done, if you look in the mirror, do you like the person you see? If you don't (or are even too tired to take a look) it's time for a time out. If you are exhausted, pooped, and out of it, it's time to *relax*. Enjoy a moment of solitude so you can restore yourself. We cannot give love, hope, and joy to others if we have none left to give.

Some of us lead lives that are so busy and so chaotic, we need to take a moment just to gather our senses. Most of us move way too fast anyway. Give yourself a chance to find out what you need to do. Be still so you can feel the peace of God as you make decisions.

If your spirit tells you to take a break, take a break. Go to the park and listen to the trees. Reconnect with nature and get grounded. Go by yourself. Remember, birds flock together, but the eagle flies alone. Get used to doing some things ALONE. It is not a curse to be alone with yourself and God.

Try this. For forty days, keep quiet about your issues. Begin with a talk diet by fasting for one day. This fast requires you speak to absolutely no one. (Of course, do this on a day when you have nothing to do). Don't answer the telephone. Don't answer the door. Talk only to God. Any issue you have will become clear to you, if you truly close your mouth and open your heart for the answer. And don't worry if you find yourself breaking this commitment; just back up and start again. Our intention here is to get grounded and appreciate the beauty of silence and the joy that comes along with it.

Enjoy the Art of Breathing

Take a deep breath. Now in this moment, stop, and feel your breath. Stop and feel the connection. Breathe deeply. Breathe slowly. Breathe consciously. The Bible reveals that when Jesus breathed on the disciples, they were filled with the power of the Holy Spirit. Likewise, your breath is your power. Breathing will keep you connected to your source of that power which is God. Breathe, knowing that you are always in the flow. Slowly, concentrate on your breath and it will do you a world of good. Breathing calms you when you are fearful, when you can't decide what to do. Breathing will keep you centered when you think you know the answer, but change your mind because you become scared. When you are afraid, stop and breathe. When there is a fire emergency, we stop, drop, and roll. In case of a spiritual emergency, we must stop, drop, and breathe. When you find yourself in the thick of it, stop, sit down, and breathe!

So, the next time you find yourself upset, stressed out, and about to go off the deep end, before you go over the top, *stop, drop, and breathe.* This is a good way to save your self from participating in a first class, whirlwind, pity-party.

Enjoy Being Your Own Cheerleader!

Go ahead. Give yourself some praise. You sure deserve it. There is nothing wrong with having a healthy sense of self-esteem. You have been giving everybody else everything for a long time. What do *you* need? What do *you* deserve? What about giving a big hooray for *you*? Get a pen and your notebook, and write down twenty ways to remind yourself that you are the best thing going since my mother's sweet potato pie! Reminding yourself of your own glory helps get you past the bumps in the road. So, go ahead. Sing your praises! I will get you started:

Hey hot stuff, you're the best!
You're looking like love to me.
Are you awesome or what?
You're a sack of sugar.
Strut your stuff.
Marvelous, you are simply marvelous.
Yes, I think you're hot!
You should put lips on the side of your face so you can kiss yourself!
Marry me! I love you.
I am blessed to know you!
You are beautiful!
Awesome, you are truly awesome.
I believe you are the one!
You are the greatest thing since pizza pie.
God broke the mold when He made you!

The list goes on and on, but I think you get the point. Cheer yourself on, every chance you get.

Enjoy Your Body

As the saying goes, *garbage in garbage out.* What you put on the inside shows up on the outside. Take care, and do not put in what will harm you. You need to be well, physically and emotionally, to live a life of power and purpose. You must have vitality. This is not possible when you eat two chocolate bars, and drink three cups of coffee a day! That depletes your energy. If you have been eating poorly, stop and feed yourself well so you will have the energy you need to live a life you love.

I know that I cannot be a great motivator, if I am not motivated myself. When I eat poorly, I feel as flat as the floor. It is simple: *I can't do well if I don't feel well.* I had to establish a health regime and stick to it. I even visited a nutritionist and had blood work done towards this end. See your doctor about an eating plan that suits you. Do some

68

form of exercise, *daily*. Go for a long walk a few times a week. Walking is stress free and easy; no fancy gym or equipment is required. Begin now to take good care of your body. Treat it well and it will treat you well.

Enjoy the Art of Play

When was the last time you did something fun and playful? Something that made you giggle with delight? (That long huh? If you can't remember, you are definitely long overdue!). Do something silly today. Lighten up! Very often I jump up and click my heels with delight just for the fun of it. I have even done cartwheels in public just because I can. The benefits of being cheerful and playing are many. Charles Dickens said, "Cheerfulness and contentment are great beautifiers, and are famous preservers of good looks."

And someone else once said, "Blessed is the one who is too busy to worry in the daytime and too sleepy to worry at night." Now that's the truth if I've ever heard it. Go have some fun. Jump on the bed. Buy a trampoline. Act silly. There is a time to work and time to play. Let's put play-time on our life agenda. Let's have a little fun.

Enjoy a Good Laugh!

Learn to laugh. Start laughing at others and yourself. My mother and I used to get a good laugh out of some of the hilarious things folk said in church. Here are some of the actual funny things we have heard:

From the pulpit, in reference to the Million Man March, the preacher made a comment on the historic event. He said, "It was one million men marching and there was not one peepa-peepa incident!" ("Peepa-peepa" was likely his use of the word "peeping" – meaning small incidents).

From the choir stand, the choir director announced to the congregation, "We gon' sing this thing without no music. We gon' do it avocado!"

An inebriated man gave advice to my younger sister, once, about how to raise her daughter. He stressed, "Remember, taking care of that baby there is primary, everything else is secretary!" Scripture is right, laughter is definitely good medicine.

Enjoy Your Friends

Good ol' friends, and good ol' shoes are just about the same: you never want to let either one of them go. There is nothing like the comfort of a pair of old shoes, which have been broken in. Likewise there is nothing like the comfort of an old friend, who knows all about you, never judges your mistakes, and keeps loving you through it all.

When you have friends who have been time tested, honored, and approved, you are blessed with abundance. Good shoes and good friends you want to keep for life. Like good shoes, good friends need to be taken care of if you want to keep them. Friends also need to be called and reminded that we love them. Be a friend to your friends and enjoy them. Call a friend, *today*, just to let him or her know how much you appreciate the friendship.

Enjoy Your Own Effort!

When you are making changes, and re-inventing your life, be sure to enjoy your own hard work. It may be difficult to be optimistic *all* the time and to stay strong, but if you are going to take the time to do something, make sure you also take time to appreciate your efforts. Make sure that what you do is fantastic. Appoint yourself the King or Queen of your chosen passion and then live it up! After all, there is no one who can do what you do, the way you can.

My secret for celebrating my efforts is to get dressed up in my baddest and best outfit and put on my make-up and some sexy shoes. Then, I stand in front of the mirror admiring myself. I give a long speech, strutting around the house like I am the best person in New York; it gives me an incredible feeling!

Once, during one of these magical moments, my friend Glenda called. She heard the excitement in my voice. I suppose she thought that some man was tickling my feet, for surely I couldn't be that excited by myself.

"What in the world are you doing?" she asked.

I paused, and then said, "I am accepting my award from the President of these United States for Outstanding Humanitarian Service!"

We cracked up! Enjoying and accepting your bigness is a fun thing to do!

Enjoy Being Patient

Being patient is not easy for me. Being patient requires that I trust life, and wait. If there is one thing God knows, it is that I do not like to wait. I want it right now, my way, and in my time. So I pray hard for patience.

Sometimes, when the answer to my prayers has not come quickly enough—I used to have a maximum wait limit of twenty minutes—I lose my patience. Nonetheless, this process of transforming my life has taught me the value of waiting. Thank God, that He knows patience and how to be gentle with us. As you re-shape your life, learn to be as

71

gentle and as patient with yourself as God is. Your time is coming. Every star has an opportunity to shine.

Enjoy Giving and Receiving Love

Once you have filled yourself up, then it is time to give to others. First, take care of yourself, love yourself, and then take that love into the world. If you find yourself becoming self-absorbed, and forgetting what matters most, that's when it's time for another time out. We can all get lost in our to-do lists. We can even get lost in the long list of things we will treat ourselves to when and if we ever finish the list of to-dos. It can be overwhelming. So before you get lost in the list, take time out to completely forget about yourself and do something good for someone else.

Whenever I feel a little blue, I know right away that I need a time out and I know what I have to do. Whenever I get the blues, it is time for me to visit someone who is sick. Somehow, sick people always minister to me. I go to brighten their spirits, but they give me truth and put me back on the path to greatness.

Once I visited a good friend who was in the hospital. He had cancer. Even though he could not walk and was lying on his back in pain, he was in the greatest of spirits. We talked for a long time. When I told him I would soon be making "Oprah" millions, he confirmed this and added, "What's for you, you ain't gonna miss. You may not get it the first time around, but you'll get it." From his hospital bed, he encouraged me and reminded me of my potential.

My friend went on and on about how marvelous I was and when he looked at me with certainty, I knew he wanted only the best for me. He had no doubt that he would be my driver. Furthermore, he told me he wanted a great salary and a tuxedo for every day of the week! (No sense in wearing the same tux twice in one week). His optimism was infectious. In that moment, my spirit was renewed. I gave him my time and he gave me hope for my future.

Giving is the real gift. When you give of your time, you receive satisfaction and love in return. Helping others helps us to help ourselves. This is love in action. Mother Teresa once said, "Love has no meaning if it isn't shared. Love has to be put into action. You have to love without expectation, to do something for love itself, not for what you may receive. If you expect something in return, then it isn't love, because true love is loving without conditions and expectations."

When we step outside of our day-to-day drama, and get about the business of helping, supporting, and loving others, we are blessed in ways we could never imagine. When we allow ourselves to be a living example of love, expressing God's goodness everyday, that too is love in action.

Practice love in action everyday; especially when you don't feel like it, and just watch your life turn around.

Enjoy the Perfect Presence of God

Always remember that God is in charge. Act like it. Rest in his presence. God will show you exactly what to do and when to do it. Stop driving yourself nuts with indecision and worry. You are God's special child.

Affirmation

I will be loving and kind,
even when I don't feel like it.
Today I will remain open to love,
so that I may serve with a full heart.
Today, I experience joy.
I will remember that kind words bring the light of God's
love into my life and the lives of others.

Prayer

Dear God:
When I am too hard on myself and want it all, *right
now*, I ask for patience as I learn how to be strong. I
now remember that everything You have promised will
come at the perfect time. As I wait, thank You for this
joyous moment. Thank You for my life. Thank You that
I am able to freely give and receive love. Thank You
that I am now fully present in all of my relationships.
As I co-create with You, God, I have prosperous,
positive experiences. Even those experiences that are
character-building have a purpose. I will count them as
joy. In Jesus' name. Amen.

SECRET TEN

BE GRATEFUL FOR WHAT YOU HAVE

*"When you wake up in the morning
and you see the sun shining
and you see the rainbow,
you better get happy!"*

—Jada Nicole Cheek, 3 years old

Are you paying attention to the good things that are in your life right now? Are you grateful for what you have? Do you consistently count your blessings? Sure, things could be a lot better, but remember, they could also be a lot worse. In her book *Simple Abundance*, Sara Ban Breathnach, suggests that we keep a daily journal and note the things we are grateful for. She calls it a Gratitude Journal. Ever consider starting one? What five things are you grateful for right now? Go ahead. Write down five things in your life that you are grateful for.

I believe that when we become grateful for the little things, God gets happy, and we set the energy in motion to appreciate the big things when they show up. Get excited— right now! Don't wait until the kids grow up and move out. There are no guarantees in life. Don't think you'll only be happy when you graduate and obtain your degree. It might take years to do that. Why put off your happiness? This is your life. You decide whether you will be happy or not. You decide if this is one of the best days of your life. You decide if these are the sweetest days you've known, and today may be all you have. None of us have contracts guaranteeing tomorrow.

Les Brown once talked about visiting a woman in the hospital who was terminally ill, but still full of vitality in her spirit and happy to be alive. When he asked her how she was doing, she said, "Better than good and better than most." Now that is gratitude for you. If this woman could be grateful, given her dire medical condition, those of us in good health should be singing for joy.

In her monthly column in *O magazine*, Oprah Winfrey said that, once, she was sobbing uncontrollably, sitting in the bathroom with the door closed while on the telephone with her spiritual mother, Maya Angelou. She said Maya Angelou told her, "Stop it! Stop it right now and say thank you." Oprah said she did not know what she was saying *thank you* for, but Maya said, "You are saying *thank you* because your faith is so strong that you don't doubt that whatever the problem, you'll get through it. You're saying thank you because even in the eye of the storm, God has put a rainbow in the clouds. You're saying thank you because you know that there's no problem created that can compare to the Creator of all things…" She's right. Start saying *thank you*. Adopt an attitude of gratitude.

Having an attitude of gratitude means you don't worry because you know things will always work out. You know that even when the storm clouds of life pass over your head, God always has an umbrella to cover you. My Dad knows about having an attitude of gratitude, whether times are good or bad. He has a saying that keeps him going. He says, "Hooooooooooray, for whatever it is!" (Emphasis on the hooray!). He simply chooses not to worry about things. If you want to operate with more power, stop worrying about things and get happy. This does not mean you walk around in denial, ignoring your problems. Just stop worrying so much about them. Take the focus off of what is wrong and look at what is right. Whatever will be will be. Let it be. Leave the troubles alone. Start being happy and grateful for the good you have in your life today.

Affirmation

I will remember that I always have everything I need and more.
I will remember that I am always in the right place at the right time.
I will remember that God constantly works on the divine plan for my life—even when it looks like He is taking a coffee break. I will not judge my life by appearances. I will live by the promises God has placed in my heart. I will continue to pursue my dream, and I am grateful for things in my life right now.

Prayer

Dear God: There are days when I have been ungrateful, when I complained too much, and prayed too little.
But today, I want You to know that I am happy *just because—just because*
You surround me with people, who are angels right here on earth. And You always put me where I need to be. This life journey is a good one.
I am happy *just because* You keep sending me little signs letting me know You are still taking care of me: pennies on the sidewalk, butterflies on the leaves, and even strangers who smile at me with joy.
I give thanks that You never forget me.
Thank You for plenty of food on my table and bills that are paid. Thank You for the abundance of family and friends, for all of their laughter and all of Your love. I am happy where I am and I am grateful.
Thank You. I pray this gratitude prayer in the name of Jesus. Amen.

SECRET ELEVEN

DON'T MISS THE LIFE LESSONS

The solution to whatever challenge we face is always the same: Don't give your power to panic.
Stand firmly in the faith that God rides on the heavens to help you. That's what God does. The divine pattern is always in place. So, lean not on your own understanding, but know that things fall apart so God can give you something better and make more of you.

—Susan L. Taylor
Publication Director
Essence Magazine

The old folk say, "If you live long enough, Maude is gonna get you." When I first heard this saying I thought who in the heck is Maude? The only Maude I knew about was the name of a television show in the seventies. I later learned that "Maude" represents life and the saying means that a long life will teach you well.

Author Gary Zukav refers to life as Life School—a place where we learn to grow through our experiences. In life then, we will receive knowledge all the time. The university called Life is constantly showing and teaching us what to do and what not to do. When we fully understand the lessons, we are promoted. If we do not fully comprehend the lessons, we experience the lessons all over again. This is not punishment. This is practice. We may often need to experience a particular life lesson again and again to master it. That repetition is God really wanting us to get life right.

We are all in Spiritual Life School, learning lessons and evolving into the powerful beings we are meant to be. Life School is on our side. It is not designed for students to fail.

Thus, reviewing your Life School notes periodically is a good practice. If you forget to review your notes, Life School will assist you in the review with a life experience.

Of course, sometimes the review comes disguised.

I fully understood this when one day, I went to the bank and wanted to shoot the bank teller. While in the bank, I completely forgot Life School lesson number one: *Remember your divine nature in all circumstances.* (Lesson number two, of course, is that students in Spiritual Life School should never shoot bank tellers!). While in the bank, I forgot that I had defined myself as a master motivational speaker, and a powerful children's storyteller who empowers others to live full, rich lives. It is challenging to walk in the spiritual truth of who you really are when people push your buttons, but that's the purpose of the life challenge: to remind you of your divine nature when it's crunch time.

I needed a certified check from my bank. This particular branch I was in was not the branch where I opened my account, so none of my paperwork was on file there. I did not have my checkbook with me, nor did I have my personal bankcard. I went to the information desk for assistance. At the information desk, a bank representative filled out a bank's check for $5,000, approved it, and sent me to a teller to cash it. However, when I got to the teller's window and the teller pulled my account up on the screen, she told me there was an alert on my account. Then, she just walked away-with no explanation at all.

When I do not get good customer service, I become very irritated. I started thinking "Doesn't she know who I am? How could she just walk away from me?" I continued to wait while the customers behind me were becoming noticeably annoyed, and I was getting more and more upset.

That is when spiritually enlightened me had the bright idea to lean over the teller's counter and move the teller's computer screen so I could look at it. Slowly, carefully, I leaned all the way over the counter. Another teller yelled at me, "You can't look at that! What's the matter with you! You can't do that!"

One would think that I didn't know that leaning over the counter in the bank, appearing as if I might be taking money out of a teller's drawer, was not problematic. So, I said, "Why not? Just why not? It's my account!" (I was livid and definitely not being very spiritual). Then I said, "Listen, go back there and get the teller who was assisting me. Tell her to get back out here. Now!" (My blood was coming to a slow boil). After she left, I stood there and waited and waited. And then I waited some more.

After what seemed to be the longest five minutes I have ever experienced in New York, the teller who had the nerve to tell me not to lean over the counter returned.

"She'll be back in a few minutes," was what the teller said. That was it! Clearly this woman did not know who she was messing with, and I still did not know what the problem was.

When you are in the bank waiting for your money, and there is a problem getting it, you start to think crazy thoughts. You can forget who you are. You do not remember anything about Spiritual Life School, or the new and dynamic person you are becoming on the road to living with purpose and power. The last thing you are thinking about is living a life you love. Thoughts enter your brain like, *the IRS has frozen my account, someone tinkered with the computer system and took all of my money out of my account, and now I will have to come back and rob the bank to get my money.* By now I was ready to strangle the teller, and return later and blow up the bank!

Totally fried, I had the bright idea to return to the information desk and get someone else to help me. I did remember one spiritual thing about Life School: *Lesson number two is really this, don't forget to breathe.* So I started breathing very slowly at first, and then more concentrated by the minute.

I spoke to a different representative at the information desk, and after our conversation she made a call to find out exactly what was going on. She then told me, "Well, Miss, the other representative should have told you that since this is not your branch, and you do not have your personal bankcard with you, we need a faxed copy of your signature card in order to cash your check. It will take a while for your branch to send the card over here."

At this point it was time to put the fork in me, because I was done! I began venting, right there in the middle of the bank. "I've been in the bank all this time, and no one told me that? What's the matter with this place? You could have at least told me what was going on, and you could have asked me to sit down and wait! I'm taking all of my money out of this institution! Where's the courtesy, where are your manners?"

"Where's the deputy manager of this bank? I demanded, "I want him or her to know about this sham of a scam you guys have going on here!"

She quietly said, "It's the Executive Branch Manager, Miss, and I will get her for you."

My very sarcastic *I'm-sick-of-all-of-you-don't-mess-with-me* response was, "Whatever!"

Instead of waiting to see the Executive Branch Manager, I decided to return to the disappearing teller. The voice in my head said, *she needs to know who I am. She can't do that to me! She needs to know who she's messing with. She cannot do that to me. Not ME!* On the way back to the teller's window, I had the distinct thought that this was a stupid idea, but my brain separated from my feet and they just kept me moving forward.

I got to the window and I asked for the $5,000 check back. The teller said that she could not give it back to me and added, "Oh, and by the way, when you first came to my counter you had an attitude."

Now my blood was boiling for sure. What did my attitude have to do with anything? I leaned my spiritually enlightened, chest heaving self back from the counter, put on my best George Foreman stance, lowered my voice an octave, and clutched my pocketbook. (I was ready to beat her in the head with that bag). With one fist up gesturing for effect and the purse in my other hand, I said, "You'll give it to me or you will meet me outside! Come on with it! You feel froggy—leap!"

At that point, she ran top speed for the supervisor, who quickly came and told me that they would rip the check up for me. (I guess I made my point).

After all of this, I finally went to the Executive Branch Manager and blasted her about how rude and nasty the teller was. I ranted on and on wondering if anyone in that bank knew the meaning of customer service? I said there are five letters in the word service that they obviously need to know—S-E-R-V-E. I noted that they were there to serve, but they were sure doing a poor job of it. The Branch Manager apologized profusely and somehow managed to calm me down.

It took me a little time to come back to my senses. She again politely apologized and said the signature card was in. As she reviewed my information, she looked at me and slowly asked, "Now, about this company of yours, who are you and what do you do?"

Suddenly, I became very quiet. (Talk about being embarrassed. This was my moment of truth). As my behavior played like a bad movie in front of me, I sheepishly said, "I am a motivator. I teach people how to live powerfully and live in joy. I know you would not believe it, based upon what happened here today."

All I could do was chuckle and hang my head in shame. We both found the whole thing amusing and laughed together.

It was HARD for me to admit who I was at that moment because I had totally forgotten that I was a divine child of God. I forgot that it was unbecoming of a spiritual student to carry on like a fool, and try to beat up the teller with her pocketbook. I also forgot I had a choice. Here is Life School lesson number three: *We always have a choice.*

That experience taught me that tests and challenges will always come. The trick is to not get caught up in them, to decide which ones are worth fighting for and which ones to let go.

The forth life lesson is: *Problems are the doorway to solutions.* Growing into your power means that you will be tested to live what you speak. So whoever you say you are, or desire to become, you will be given a contrasting experience to help you become that kind of person. For example, the contrast for peace is often an experience of chaos, so aspiring to become a peacemaker requires one to face some frustration. If you say you desire to be financially free and in order, you may face a financial emergency. The contrast for financial prosperity may be dire financial straits, or even bankruptcy. Life gives you the experience of what you *don't* want, so you can create what you *do* want.

For example, at one point in my life, I was walking around affirming, "I am love and truth. Love constantly surrounds me." I was just a happy love-bug bouncing around. All of a sudden, I was dealing with a most unloving experience and I learned the fifth, great Life Lesson: *People come into our lives to teach us.*

When I moved into the Co-op, one morning at seven a.m. my neighbor downstairs rang my doorbell. When I opened the door, she angrily said, "Yesterday, there was a crash, boom, bang, boom, and all kinds of noises coming from this apartment. I did not like it!"

I was surprised by her tone of voice, her boldness, and even her look. She looked crazy, so that's the name I gave her: Crazy. I was also upset because, at seven o'clock in the morning, you do not expect to see Crazy looking crazy and talking crazy at your front door!

With my New York attitude of indignation I said, "I'm moving in, do you mind?"

She didn't blink, but just continued complaining about the noise and the boom, bang, boom stuff...not a good start for new neighbors.

The next day, Crazy brought a bottle of champagne upstairs and gave it to me. That seemed to be the end of the matter, but it was not. She always had a problem with the slightest bit of noise, from me banging nails into the walls to just plain talking. I think that if I passed gas and she heard it, she would have called the police. Nonetheless, I tried to understand Crazy's point of view. She hadn't had a neighbor living upstairs over her head for over a year, and the floors in the apartment were very thin. Yet still, over time, the situation grew ever more difficult.

On Christmas day, I decided to put my "LOVE" thing to work. I had been professing it, so now I would live it. I decided to be sweet and loving to everybody, *especially Crazy.* That's when I went downstairs to invite her to my party. Let me be clear here. Spirit (the little voice inside) told me *not* to go downstairs. But I was so busy trying to be *right* that I did not acknowledge that voice. (Have you ever heard a voice in your head telling you NOT to do something…and you did it anyway?).

When I arrived downstairs, Crazy gave me a Christmas ornament from her tree. Then I politely told her I was having a party and there would be music playing. She said, "Well, there has been music playing all day, but you can play your music because we won't be here." That is what she said, but what I heard was Crazy (with an attitude) granting me permission to play my own music in my own apartment.

"Oh, I am going to play it!" I said sarcastically.

Crazy's boyfriend was there and he said, "You see! You see! That is why you *cannot* be friends with her. You can't. I told you, you just can't. She's crazy!"

Then he turned to me and yelled, "You keep making all this noise, and I'll put a thing up to the ceiling. I'll give you noise alright!"

If I thought Crazy was crazy, her boyfriend was off the wall! Looking at Dumb and Dumber, I said, "I resent what you're saying and you can take back this little funky

Christmas ornament you gave me!" I threw it down on the floor and I walked off!

When I got back to my apartment, I went into my bedroom and started praying. "It appears to me, Lord, that I am dealing with Crazy, and I need a heavenly remedy for this earthly problem right now."

Perhaps, when *you* ask God for something, *you* don't expect the answer immediately, but I sure do. So, twenty angry minutes later, when I did not hear anything from God, I said, "Well Lord, since You have not yet responded, You know that I am willing to help You work Your mojo with this one." ("Mojo," by my definition, is my effort to help God out and be God junior. However, it has ALWAYS resulted in a mess!).

My thought was that I just want to scare my neighbor, that's it. So, I took my happy hips downstairs, and first started praying outside of Crazy's door. Then I snapped. I said, "I curse you. I curse you. I curse you!" I was so mad I started speaking in my version of tongues. "A shing-a-ling, a-ling, a shing-a-ling, a-ling!" I said this, shaking my index finger at the door.

(And this is the behavior of a spiritually enlightened woman?).

As if that was not enough, I put some leaves, and a few matches, by the door for effect. I knew this was wrong and definitely <u>not</u> the Christian thing to do, but I was too caught up in my emotions to think straight. I have no clue what this was supposed to do; I was just working the *mojo* remember? I was helping God out. I left, went upstairs, and laughed my head off!

About two weeks later, I received a notice from the Internal Affairs Division of the Co-op. They wanted to meet with me about a "situation" with a fellow tenant. I know it makes no sense but that's when I became upset with God. I was the one who created the confusion and then had the nerve to be upset with God. Why was I being summoned to this meeting? Did we not agree, God, I was helping You out? I was working the mojo remember? What was I to do, lay hands on myself? On and on I went.

I went to the meeting with a friend. I wore my best attorney suit, and carried a big accordion folder and briefcase with nothing in it. (I still know the value of looking like a brilliant attorney!). After Crazy presented her side of the story, it was my turn to speak: I lied with the utmost sincerity, laced with righteous indignation. "I have absolutely no idea what you are talking about. I am even appalled that you would think I would put something by your door. However, I understand. If someone would have done that to me, I would be here too." Me being right, and looking good, meant more to me than some old affirmation about being truth and love.

When we left the meeting, my friend asked me, "What in the world was she talking about? What stuff by the door? What was that all about?"

After I explained it all, he said, "You are crazy!"

And he just kept saying it over and over and over. "You are crazy. You ARE crazy. YOU ARE CRAZY."

That made me think. If I am crazy, then maybe I AM Crazy. Maybe I am just like Crazy. Remember, in Secret Eight, the Aborigines of Australia say, "Self and others are one." So if I truly was crazy, what was I saying, as Crazy, to myself? If people come into your life to teach you things, then what was my neighbor, Crazy, teaching me?

One thing Crazy kept saying loud and clear was that, *there was too much noise upstairs.* She kept saying that I *made too much noise up there.* She kept requesting silence. It took me a little while to get it, but I finally got it. *There was too much noise up there in my own head! I needed to be silent. It was time to take it easy for a while. I had to take a minute, be still, and definitely stop making so much noise.* She didn't know it, but Crazy really was trying to tell me something. My situation with Crazy ended up creating access to a solution with my own problems; she truly had to come teach to me something.

After the Crazy incident, I was ready to pack up and move; however, I remembered that it is imperative not to run away when you are being tested. Sit with the test for a minute. Get what life is showing you, so you don't miss the lesson.

People really do come to teach us. Look at the people in your life. What are your issues with them? Now, turn it around and see if that is your issue with yourself. The answers to your issues are all around you. Right in the middle of my problem, there was my solution—and Crazy was telling me what to do about it. I had to just stop and hear the message. There was too much noise going on for me to hear it. I had all kinds of thoughts going on in my own head. I needed to stop making noise outwardly, with my uncensored mouth and unpredictable behavior, and quiet myself inwardly so that I could hear the answers. When we stop making noise about what is happening outside of us, we really can learn a lot from the people who are inside our world.

Finally, here are ten tips that will help you with Life School:

1. Spiritual Life School teaches you lessons about life, and how to master the human experience.
2. It's a good idea to do all of the required course work, if you want to graduate with honors.
3. Should you decide to skip some of the work, you will have to repeat the life lesson and relive the drama again.
4. Before you advance to another level, there will be tests. The best students, of course, get the hardest tests.
5. You are given everything you need to know to pass. Expect a few pop quizzes on things like fear, courage, patience, and faith.
6. Study your notes daily. Practice makes things almost perfect.
7. If you forget to study your notes, or become too lazy to review them and wish to quit this course, I strongly advise you to remain, pray, and press on.
8. Each course is for you. At any time, you may exercise free will and withdraw. This, of course, does not stop Life from handing out more tests and experiences.
9. When you feel tested, *breathe* before you respond. If you forget to breathe, and you go forward and fall down, you can get back up. Remember that the prayer line is open 24 hours a day, 7 days a week for your convenience.
10. Upon graduation, you will receive a degree. This entitles you to even more advanced Spiritual Life School work.

Affirmation

I will pass every test.
I will pass every test.
I will pass every test.

Prayer

Lord, I need Your guidance and wisdom to see me
through. I realize that You are a God of clarity and
direction, and that you do not need my help.
So, I pray that You will sit in my heart
and shower me with the light of understanding. I pray
that when I move, I will know exactly which way to go.
Breathe on me; help me understand what You are
teaching me at all times and in all situations.
I thank You for helping me master the lessons of
Life School. Thank You for giving me the power to turn
my life around. Thank You for each opportunity I have
had to put into practice all that I have learned.
Thank You for my wonderful, new life that spills over
with power and purpose.
I am "Divine Purpose in Action," and I am grateful.
I pray these things in the name of Jesus. Amen.

SECRET TWELVE

FORGIVE YOURSELF

And be ye kind to one another, tenderhearted, forgiving one another, even as God for Christ's sake hath forgiven you.

—Ephesians 4:32

To be who you are and become what you are capable of is the only goal worth living.

—Alvin Ailey

When I was young, Mom had to work the night shift at the bank. From ten o'clock at night to six o'clock in the morning, she was away from my two younger sisters and I. She worked nights for the increase in salary. Earning more money meant she could do better for our family. But, she had to leave us alone…a lot.

True, there were neighbors who checked in on us, but what I vividly remember is that no one was there when it became dark. I remember being scared to death that someone would break in and harm us, that the howling wind was really an intruder, or that the building would catch on fire. These were frightening experiences for an eleven-year old child. (To this day, I am still afraid of the dark). At the time, I never revealed how afraid I was, and how much I wished my mother could stay home with us. I was trying to be a "big girl." I also held onto being upset with my mother about it for years.

When I was upset, I thought I could have done a better job parenting than my mother did. The truth is that I would have done far worse. I would have been a basket case taking care of three children. I have no children yet; I just have fish. And some days, I don't even remember to feed the fish! I hate changing their water and the filter stays filthy. At other times, I have even forgotten not only where I parked my car, but that I even drove it to work in the first place! I have driven in to work, parked the car in the municipal parking lot, and then walked right past the lot at the end of the day only to take the bus home, remembering the car the next day.

When I got out of my self-righteous, angry shoes, I realized that I could not have done a better job than my Mom did. Mom raised three young girls by working the night shift, and we wanted for nothing. A few years ago, I apologized to my mother for making her wrong. I said goodbye to all my anger and guilt toward her, and ended up with one of the best doses of freedom I have ever tasted.

Whatever keeps you in emotional bondage, I challenge you to let it go. But, how, you ask? How do I let go and forgive?

One way to release anger is to write a letter. (Writing is a great way to release whatever is bugging you, and it is a crucial part of the forgiveness process). Write directly to the person you are angry with. Give it all you've got! They deserve to be told off! Start with, "I am angry with you because..." Then when you have finished stating what you are angry about add, "I am willing to forgive you because... Or, I am willing to let this go because..."

You may, or may not, want to mail the letter when you complete it. In fact, you may want to destroy it. Do what feels right for you. Do not worry if you are not ready to write this letter right now. Step by step, issue-by-issue, this is how we walk the path to live a life we love.

Forgiving others requires being brave, and the transformation is worth it. Stepping up and being brave enough to forgive someone is an act of courage.

I remember, once, how I stayed angry with a group of people from my former church for a long time. I was so angry that I wanted to kill the folk who upset me, including the minister! I imagined telling God, You know that little issue I have been praying about? Well, no need to solve it because I took care of it for Ya!

My pride did not allow me to let go of my anger. Once again, I was committed to being right. In my mind, I *was* right and the church folk were wrong and did not deserve my forgiveness. But forgiveness is not for us; it is a gift *for* giving.

Not being totally clear on the value and necessity of forgiveness, I was so upset that I put the "Miss Celie" curse—from the movie, "The Color Purple"—on the church folk. In the movie, Miss Celie put up her right hand and extended her index and middle fingers to Mister (the man who had abused her for years). "Until you do right by me," Miss Celie said, "everything you touch is going to crumble – everything you think about is going to fail!" Ms. Celie held "Mister" emotionally hostage, and now I was doing the same thing to the church people. I even felt justified all of my outrageous actions. I did not want to let go of being upset. I did not want to forgive.

Why? It is hard to let things go when you think you are right! And if you are a person who can be controlling like me, it will be even harder to surrender being upset (especially when you *know* you are right!). Controllers want things their way, in their time, and on their terms. Like most controlling people, I wanted people to do what I wanted done, when I wanted it done. I have also been known to have fits. Sometimes, I didn't act like a sane person during these fits of control. I did what felt good, what felt right, and what I thought made sense—in the moment. That's why I put the Miss Celie curse on the church folk. And when they did not get the mortgage they were trying to get, I confess I nearly laughed myself silly. I let revenge run away with me.

Eventually I forgave them—two years later! It took that long time for me to see how ridiculous I was acting. But, the real truth was that I was making myself crazy with anger. Anytime I saw one of the church people, my stomach became tied in knots. When I finally I let it go, my whole body relaxed.

Mastering the art of forgiveness, for me, starts when I acknowledge the truth of what is going on, when I stop doing things my way, and when I stay open to something new. That's surrender. The garden of surrender opens up when we understand that, no matter what happens, God will take care of us. And because I no longer wanted to experience those knots in my stomach, I *had* to let it go.

Forgiveness goes hand in hand with surrender. Real forgiveness means you surrender and give it to God; you let go of control. Surrender is the art of letting go and giving your frustration, anxiety, and anger over to God. Surrender allows you to let events unfold, as they should. Scripture teaches us not to seek vengeance because vengeance belongs to God: He will repay. When you surrender your anger, you allow the spiritual law of *what goes around comes around* to unfold.

If forgiving someone else is not your issue, perhaps it is yourself that could stand a little forgiving. The healing power of forgiveness casts out all guilt and shame. Forgiving ourselves is also a brave, bold action to take. We have not completed the forgiveness process if we forgive the other person, and do not forgive ourselves. Forgiveness is taking a close look into the mirror of our souls, and being honest about what we have done. It is hard to do, but again necessary.

How do you forgive yourself? I don't have all the answers to that one. I do know that one way to begin is the same way we forgive others. Write a letter...*to yourself.* I wrote a forgiveness letter to myself. In this letter, I wrote down the good, the bad, and the ugly—exactly how I felt about myself. I started with, "Dear Tonya, I am angry with you because...I have not treated you well because..." If you choose to write a letter to yourself, acknowledge what you feel—all of it. Be completely truthful. Acknowledging that you need forgiveness is just the first step, for forgiveness is a two-fold process.

Next is actually asking for forgiveness. The process is not complete until you ask the other person (or yourself) for forgiveness. Even if they do not forgive you right away, you know that you have made an effort. If the person chooses not to forgive you, it is okay. You have created a space for forgiveness and healing, and that is what God requires.

My letter continued with, "Today, I am willing to forgive you. Today, I begin the process of letting you off the hook. Today, I acknowledge that I have not had such a great relationship with you, but from this point on, I will." Use your own words to accept that you forgive yourself.

When you are finished, sign your letter, date it, and then destroy it. Burn the paper, or tear it into tiny pieces, as a symbol of letting it all go. Or, you may choose to mail it to yourself and open it at a much later date. This may be an emotional, uneasy, and unsettling letter to write. Coming face to face with our shortcomings is never easy. That's okay. Remember this is a process. It may not feel great to you right now, but if you can sit with it and do it, you will feel an emotional release and the shackles of unforgiveness will be broken.

Another way to forgive your self is to use the power of the spoken word. Find a safe, quiet space and slowly repeat the following prayer out loud:

For not listening to my life and God's direction the first time,
I forgive myself,
For ever believing that I was dirty and could not be forgiven,
I forgive myself.
For staying stuck in a place that did not represent the true me,
I forgive myself.
For going back again and again
to that place that did not represent the true me,
I forgive myself.
For being angry with myself,
for missing the lesson and the blessing the first time,
I forgive myself.
For not being prepared,
I forgive myself.
For asking God to turn on my light and then turning it off again,
I forgive myself.
For not telling the truth when I was supposed to,
I forgive myself.
For being undisciplined and disobedient,
I forgive myself.
For being too hard on myself,
I forgive myself.
For all the times I did not see myself
as the beautiful child of God that I am,
I forgive myself.
For competing with others
when I know there is more than enough for us all,
I forgive myself.
For opening my big mouth when I could have shut up,
I forgive myself.
For asking for it and then not wanting it,
I forgive myself.
For harming my body,

I forgive myself.
For not speaking my truth when I could have,
and lowering my standards just because I wanted to be loved,
I forgive myself.

AND FOR ANYTHING ELSE
that I may do in the future that does not reflect my true
purpose, and is not an image of the likeness of God in me,
I forgive myself.

After you are finished pardoning yourself, you have planted the spiritual seeds of forgiveness. The words of forgiveness you speak will grow into the reality of your experience. If the hurt feelings do not disappear over night, know that things must form in a spirit seed first, before they sprout in the physical realm. Writing down, acknowledging, and then forgiving whatever you are angry about, opens the way for the Creator to meet you where you are. You will begin to know that you really are forgiven and that you truly have forgiven someone else. Then you will be able to act out that belief of freedom, rather than fear.

Most importantly, please know that God is not upset with you! God is never angry because we have messed up. Actually, our "messing up" gives God the chance to help us see how far we have strayed from our purpose. In time the mess will age to give us the message. "Messing up" ought to make us wise. It is an opportunity to hear God loud and clear. Messing up is a blessing in disguise, because it gives us a good reason to straighten out our affairs, and puts us back on the path to a life we love.

I cannot tell you *every* single personal step you need to take so that you are well on your way to living a purposeful life of power. I will tell you that you cannot accomplish it by yourself, I didn't. All along the way, God sent angels to assist me, and He energized me with the power of His Holy Spirit to pull me onward when things got tough. With a lot of prayer and work, by the grace of God, you too can walk in your destiny. I will also tell you that one day, you will be busy minding your own business and whoosh! You'll get it! All of the steps you have taken to transform your life will take effect and you will know that you are living in a new place - a place where you are living a life you love!

Final Thoughts

There is a power that lies deep within all of us. It is the power that allows us to soar to unimaginable heights. It is the power that pushes us onward when we feel like giving up. It is the power of God. Tap into this power when you feel weighed down with issues, when the going gets tough. You must hold on! Especially when you think you cannot, when you think you have nothing left. This is exactly when your breakthrough is coming!

Summon up your courage and say, *I can do it!* If you become faint of heart, go back, rework your plan, and try something new. Remember that your faith is always bigger than your "I can't." Things may not be easy. Things may get a little rough at times, but accept the truth that God has endowed you with everything you need to prosper. This is your time. Go forth and prosper. You are prepared enough, equipped enough, and bold enough! Now is the time to step up to a life you love!

TONYA KERRI JOHNSON is an attorney who has practiced as both a defense attorney and a prosecutor. After many years in the legal arena, Tonya decided to give it all up and pursue her passion for speaking. Today, Tonya has become a dynamic speaker and teacher who delivers a high-energy message challenging people to soar! Her lectures are so spirit-filled and exciting that she has affectionately been named, "The Queen of Fire!" Tonya Kerri Johnson has dedicated her life to inspiring others and coaching them to excellence.

For more information on Tonya Kerri Johnson and her motivational programs, products, and services, write or call:

Tonya Kerri Johnson
P.O. Box 202
Burlington, NJ 08016

(866) 647-7734 PIN # 6090 (Toll Free)